WHEN THE WAR IS OVER
...A NEW ONE BEGINS

Rebuilding Relationships After Trauma

WHEN THE WAR

IS OVER
...A NEW ONE BEGINS

**Rebuilding
Relationships After Trauma**

CHUCK DEAN AND BETTE NORDBERG

WordSmith [WS] *Publishing*
Seattle, Washington 98168

When the War Is Over...A New One Begins

Published by WordSmith Publishing, P.O. Box 68065, Seattle, WA 98168.

Cover Design by Terrence Broadus & Broad-Minded Graphics
Interior design by Pine Hill Graphics

ISBN: 0-9727279-3-0

Printed in the United States of America.

Table of Contents

INTRODUCTION

I (Chuck Dean) have often wondered how two people ever write a book together—especially two creative, strong-willed writers who are accustomed to doing it their way. Well, I finally found out, and it has not been as painful as I suspected. Writing with Bette has been a genuine treat and a growing experience for me.

Not long after reading her novel *Serenity Bay* something began to stir in my heart about her style and burden for people suffering from abuses in life. When she asked me for technical advice on her novel *Thin Air*, I knew we could work together.

Days after terrorists attacked the United States, in September 2001, the idea for this book was birthed in my heart. I felt that more than ever the world needed a good solid approach to building better relationships after trauma. I could have written a one-author view, but something urged me to step out on a limb and invite Bette to write it with me.

I knew that a book on relationships desperately needed both a male and female perspective. My instincts were right—after all, who wants to hear some guy talk about relationships? I am so happy that she accepted (also stepping out on a limb), and you will see why when you read what we have jointly put to paper.

As you read this book, you'll notice that we've chosen to write in a single voice. We didn't want to confuse you or distract you with guessing, *who is writing now?* You can read the whole text as though I wrote it myself. But you can be very certain that Bette's keyboard has been all over it.

You might be surprised to know that when I think of relationships, I think of more than the relationships between men and women, or husbands and wives. Some of the best relationships in my life are those I share with friends.

I learned a lesson a couple of years ago when my wife decided she wanted a divorce because of a church doctrine disagreement. For once in my life I did not immediately run from the situation but tried everything in my power to reconcile with her. I was shunned by the fellowship of our church and lost contact with six family members, including two grandbabies. However, in spite of my determined efforts, she proceeded with the split, and I was forced out.

Needless to say, I was devastated. It felt worse than losing my buddies in Vietnam. My family hadn't died; I just couldn't see them or talk to them. I don't think I ever blamed God, but for the first time I had doubts about being a Christian. As each day passed, I felt my heart growing colder.

Not many days after this tragic event, the Lord intervened. An old friend called and invited me to the Point Man meeting on Tuesday nights. Though Bob Silveria and I had worked together in Seattle before, I had not been to a veterans' meeting for years. Bob is a true brother in the Lord and a fellow paratrooper, so naturally we share lots of common ground.

In a haze of emotions, I began to attend, and these men, these warriors of the faith, embraced me and began to help carry my burden. Their prayers and love brought me along, and my faith was restored. And through it all God has shown me many valuable lessons that I may never have learned otherwise.

As I was thinking about this whole set of circumstances the other day, I felt humbled by the amount of restoration and healing that came into my life through this bonding. I was then reminded of an analogy I once heard about a bonfire.

When a burning ember pops out of a bonfire and becomes separated from the heat of the fire, it doesn't take long for the ember to grow cold. However, if you take that cold piece of charcoal and return it to the still red-hot embers of the fire, the cold one will once again become bright-hot like the others.

As I attended those meetings, I realized that these men would give up their lives for me. Through Bob's dedication to serve the Lord, his friendship and trust, I was able to feel accepted and whole again. That is what a good relationship can do for you. It can turn your black coal into a burning ember.

Relationships help us handle life. When people have good friends to support them, they handle stressful situations more easily. This comes home to me each time I attend a veteran's meeting where men and women support one another on the journey to healing.

When we experience trauma, too many of us feel that the bridges connecting us to the rest of the world have been burned. We wallow in the resulting isolation, afraid of what others might think if they really knew, afraid to reach out, afraid to ask for the help we need. Our fear convinces us to sever all remaining ties, and we build rock walls to keep us safe from the rejection we fear most. Alone, we grow cold. We lose our joy. And we lose hope.

You don't have to lose hope. The help is out there. You will find it in relationships.

AND BETTE SAYS:

I met Chuck Dean by telephone several years ago, when he helped me with research for a novel I wrote for Bethany House Publishers. One of my characters was a Vietnam veteran, and I wanted to portray him with gentleness and understanding. I'd read Chuck's *Nam Vet* book and knew he could help me create a believable character. In the end, Chuck chose to read early drafts of the work, giving me valuable suggestions. His expertise saved me from more than one serious plotting mistake.

I was too young to care much about the Vietnam War while it happened. But I've made up for lost time. As I've worked with Chuck I learned much, and before long, I found a new compassion for many veteran's issues.

So, when Chuck came to me with the idea for this book, I saw it as one small contribution that I might make to the valiant men who fought for our country.

But I had other motives too.

I grew up as the only girl in a family of five boys. I knew what it felt to be a Venetian living on planet Mars. My mother dressed me in ruffles, and my brothers put a football helmet on my head and took me outside for the game. In those days, parents were encouraged not to focus on their children. They believed that too much attention would be harmful; my father's mantra was, "Children should be seen and not heard."

He lived out the mantra by ignoring his children—until we managed to get ourselves into trouble. Then his outbursts were tyrannical and violent. I grew up hungry for his affirmation and attention, wondering if I deserved to be loved. It seemed clear that Dad didn't love me. Could anyone?

Those needs drove me and I made many unhealthy choices, some of which have affected my whole life. Interestingly though, I managed to look pretty together on the outside. I was an outstanding student, an accomplished gymnast, and social enough to join a college sorority.

But I wasn't happy.

In college, I came to a desperate place. I needed love and direction. I needed forgiveness. I chose Jesus. I made the same decision we'll speak about later in this book and I've never, not for one itty-bitty moment, regretted it. I'm writing here from a Christian worldview.

Though Jesus forgave me for all my bad decisions, he did not wipe away the history that led to them—or their lasting effects.

I came to a crisis point about ten years ago, when everything in my life seemed to fall apart. My husband and I spent a year living at different addresses. I spent several years relearning the basics about myself. That process—the reconsidering of my past and relearning my value as a person—what trendy folks have called, *finding myself*, began in a counselor's office.

But the real healing took place in relationships.

Over the past twenty years, I have cultivated a close-knit group of women friends with whom I can be totally honest. We meet informally—we walk together, we work together, we ride bikes together. Through our long history together, my friends know everything there is to know about me and choose to love me anyway. These women carry me through the bad times and celebrate with me in the good. They know my weaknesses and refuse to let me excuse myself for bad behavior.

Though we share no formal relationship, these women aren't afraid to ask the tough questions. And they wait quietly for my answers. They warn me of the dangers they see coming my way—some of which come from my own stubborn determination and some from those parts of me that are still growing into adulthood. They don't let me off the hook. It isn't easy. But their love has been the most powerful force in my life.

Often, my heavenly Father cloaks his love for me in their arms.

Their love has been painful as well. I won't imply that the road has been perfect. We've had misunderstandings. We've had to talk through some problems, but we've kept it going. For nearly twenty years, we've kept our commitments to one another alive.

I'm happy to say that my husband and I will celebrate our 28th wedding anniversary this fall. Tough relationships can get better. Love can bloom in difficult circumstances.

I have found that my connections with other people are the source of courage I need to face every day of my life.

I've heard many Christians espouse this philosophy: "When you have Jesus, you don't need anything or anyone else." I don't agree. This morning, I opened my Bible's concordance and counted sixty-one "one-another" commands. Sixty-one!

"Love one another."

"Bear one another's burdens."

"Through love, serve one another" … The commands go on and on.

Over and over, the Bible commands us to find and nurture relationships through which we can meet one another's *real* needs: physical, spiritual, emotional.

And if you think about it, those commands make a great deal of sense. If we are to consider the people in the church the body of Christ, then we are his hands, his feet, his voice. It only makes sense that he would use his body to touch us and heal us and help us. You may consider the church—those people we know and love—to be Jesus' hands and arms, loving and supporting us. Through people, God often brings us wholeness.

So, for me, relationships are not optional—they are critical. Without them, I would have lost hope long ago. If there is a single theme in all of my writing, it is this: through relationships, we experience the very best things our Creator has to offer us as humans.

I wrote to give you hope, and courage, and skills. But most of all, I wrote so that you would find what I have. Through my relationships, I'm growing into the best person I can be. I am experiencing the best my Creator has to offer.

I want that for you, dear reader, as well.

Before You Begin:

We hope that this book will help you rebuild the relationships that have been damaged by the trauma you've experienced. Whatever you've faced, be it war or flooding, terrorist attacks or a violent assault on a city street, be it a car accident, or a tornado; you can restore those relationships most precious to you. We'll show you how.

No matter what your marital status, we know that trauma affects relationships. It has a way of isolating even the most courageous of survivors. We hope our words can bring you restoration and growth. In so doing, you will experience a level of health and fulfillment you may never have believed possible.

ONE MORE THING:

Bette and I come from a Christian worldview. We've both experienced a defining moment of change in our spiritual lives. Once we saw that our own path led to destruction, we made a clear choice to follow Jesus Christ. We can no more hide our worldview than a leopard can change his spots.

The Bible has a great deal to say about relationships. In fact, the whole book is about the God of the universe seeking relationship with his creation. You are his creation. However, you need not share our spiritual perspective in order to use this material. Our suggestions are true and helpful regardless of your belief system. Spending less than you earn (a Biblical truth by the way) will eventually get you out of debt—no matter what you believe about God. In the same way, the relational skills espoused in the Bible will absolutely enhance your experiences among other humans, no matter what your faith.

TAKE NOTE OF THIS:

You'll note that I've included many statistics from other sources. In order to keep the text readable, we've left out footnotes. If you need them, the citations can be found, listed by chapter, at the end of the book.

I've included a series of important questions at the end of every chapter.

I hope these questions help you reflect on what you've read. Think about your past. Look for ways the issue has affected life since your trauma. Keep a pen nearby as you work through your thoughts. Some of you may want to start a separate notebook on the subject; you'll want to write paragraphs of reflection. For others, only a single word or name added in the margin of the book will be enough to remind you of your thoughts.

However you choose to do it, we want you to think through the issue. Have you experienced this struggle in the past? How has the struggle affected your present relationships? After some reflection you'll want to take the first step. Choose one or two small ways to practice these new ideas.

Even if you only begin to *think* differently, that is change! One small advance will bring another and another. In the end, you will have taken the hill labeled "healthy relationships." We wish you the best success!

We want to hear from you. Let us know what happens!

Chuck Dean and *Bette Nordberg*

CHAPTER ONE

Alone
in a
Crowd

*Those of us who did make it, have an obligation to teach oth-
ers what we know, and to try with what's left of our lives, to
find a goodness and meaning to this life. The war is over for
me now. But it will always be there, for the rest of my days...*
                    Platoon, screenplay by Oliver Stone

Failed suicide attempt." I heard the professional, expression-
less tone in the policeman's voice—even over the telephone
line. "He wants to see you."

With heavy heart, I hung up and drove to the hospital. I had
no idea what to expect when I opened the door to Jim's room. Of
all the veterans I knew, Jim seemed least likely to choose death
as the answer to the problems he faced.

What on earth could have brought him to this point?

As I stepped into the room, Jim mustered a sheepish smile.
His pale, tired features showed through the false front. His smile
turned to a frown when he recognized me.

"How you doin', Jim?" I pulled a chair to the bedside.

"Awful, thanks to the next door neighbor and all these f—ing people." He threw a tissue box at the wall and glared out the window.

Not sure what to say, I asked, "Did someone hurt you last night?"

He ignored the question. "All I wanted to do was die, and I couldn't even do that. I should have done it some other way—to make sure no one could keep me alive. God, I'm such a failure." Jim avoided eye contact and his voice broke as he said, "This is just another way to prove it."

The words took me by complete surprise. Jim had a beautiful wife, a great family, and a successful career. How could he consider himself a failure?

In the weeks that followed, I visited Jim whenever I could, even after he left the medical ward and entered an in-hospital, eight-week post-traumatic stress program. During those visits, I discovered some interesting things about my friend.

Jim lived two different lives.

To the outside world, Jim projected a bright and hopeful exterior. But the inner man, the one who lived inside, knew a blackness so deep he could swim in it. By strength of will, he pulled himself out of bed every day, his chest aching with depression, and moved through his obligations. Jim refused to let anyone know how he really felt. From the day he came home from Vietnam, Jim used all his energy in a kind of emotional calisthenics—desperate to keep up the deception.

As a highly disciplined Green Beret, Jim carefully separated his emotional war from his outward life. He managed to develop a highly successful business; providing well for his family.

His military training actually *enabled* him to lead two lives—one exuding strength and success—the other encumbered by depression, guilt, and fear. Jim lived like an Olympic athlete in a swimming race—swimming with all his might, anxious to beat his competitors.

Unlike the other swimmers, Jim had a serious handicap. Jim swam his race attached to a three-foot beach ball, which he kept firmly hidden under the surface of the water. When the ball threatened to pop into view, he focused on keeping it down. But the distraction and effort made Jim fall behind. Letting go of the beach ball, he would swim with all his might, desperate to catch up—until once again, his beach ball threatened to surface.

His life formed an exhausting and unproductive cycle. Swim a little, push the ball down; swim a little, push the ball down.

For thirty years, Jim managed to get through his days in a debilitating succession of playacting. Sleep brought him no comfort. Frequent nightmares created a sleep deprivation so severe and so long lasting that role playing became nearly impossible. Often, startled awake by terrorizing combat dreams, Jim moved to the computer where he spent long hours in the dead of night. His wife believed he was catching up on work. In truth, Jim used Internet chat rooms to visit with other combat veterans.

In spite of the many people in his life, Jim felt alone. Isolated. His combat experiences trapped him in an unearthly hell. Unable to connect with other people, Jim had no way of dealing with his emotional devastation. Like termites attacking the foundation of a building, eventually the damage became apparent for all to see, and Jim's carefully maintained exterior crumbled to dust. The ball finally popped out of the water, and Jim gave up the race.

Does this sound familiar?

Most combat veterans can identify with Jim's life. You are not the first to have these feelings. In fact, believing that no one else has ever felt this way, adds to the isolation most veterans experience. In truth, nearly every combat veteran faces these issues. Listen to the words of other veterans, from other wars...

> When our country decided to take the Islands back from Britain, they sent us, (mostly eighteen and nineteen-year-olds), to do the fighting. We had practically no training,

and some of us had only fired a few rounds from our weapons in preparation. We were no match for the British. Our return home was not a victorious one at all, and now I often wonder if life is worth living. Suicide seems to be the best way out of the hell I live day after day. (Argentinean soldier, Falkland War)

If I had not gone to war none of this would have happened. It has scarred me in other places besides my body. My wife would not have divorced me and I would not have lost my family. If she only knew what I went through in Afghanistan... (Russian soldier, Afghanistan War)

During these days off I retreated to my own little "foxhole," a small, dimly lit room that was filled with some old relics I brought home from the war. There I would spend time with my demons, and they would torment my mind through the memories of what I had seen and experienced in Africa. Nobody at work ever knew of my problems because I covered it up so well. I never wanted anyone to think I was crazy because of the war. (World War II veteran)

I was discharged and went silently back to my job. I was as confused as everyone else about the "police action" and not much was mentioned about it after that. At times I would feel some bitterness begin to rise up inside me...The best way for me to control any bad feelings and resentments was to work hard in the days and drink a lot at night. My wife and I became regulars at several taverns and dance halls, but my drinking became a threat to our marriage. When I would get drunk, I would either become remorseful or belligerent...I just had too much pent-up frustration and I had to release it somehow. (Korean veteran)

All of these men developed patterns of isolation. They kept their wartime involvement to themselves. Unable or unwilling to tell the truth about their past, they became a kind of secret agent, living a "false identity" in a new country.

Why were they afraid to reveal the truth? Did they fear rejection? Guilt? Were they afraid of the questions of others? Were their relationships too fragile for the horrible truth they'd experienced? Did they really believe that they could keep these secrets forever, never having to tell anyone about the personal side of war?

Why *do* veterans have difficulty with intimate relationships?

I can speak from my own experience. I served in Vietnam beginning in May of 1965 as part of the first regular army combat unit to begin escalating the 10,000 Day War. We were sent for a year into the rice paddies, jungles, and coastlines of Southeast Asia to "stop communist aggression."

When I left home, I believed that after serving in Vietnam, I would be able to come back and pick up my life exactly where I left off. It never occurred to me that my experience in Vietnam would change my life forever.

I will never forget my coming home experience:

At two o'clock in the morning the temperature in Vietnam hovered in the mid-nineties. We had turned in our weapons and equipment the previous day and were confined to a tiny barbed wire compound at the airbase. For some of us the war was over. We looked forward to boarding a jetliner and forever leaving this living hell. After drinking dozens of beers, we scrounged for a place to sleep.

I managed to find a mattress inside a small building made of corrugated tin and scrap wood and settled in to relax for the few hours before our plane would leave. Moments later, just as I'd begun to slip into a drunken stupor, a frightening but familiar sound blasted me into consciousness. Incoming mortar explosions violently rocked the small compound.

Instinctively, I threw the mattress over me as the air-bursting explosions ripped through the area. Pounding my fists into the ground, I screamed in anger, "You're not going to get me now! I'm going home! You're not getting me now!"

As suddenly as it began, the explosions ceased. I heard the injured crying out. Nearby, someone screamed at a dead friend, ordering him to get up. I ran to a wounded soldier, his stomach gashed open, and ripped off my shirt. As I applied it to the wound, I shouted for a medic.

Seven teenage soldiers died that morning in a tiny compound ten thousand miles from home. After spending one year in the hell of Vietnam, this was their reward. How unjust it seemed!

By the time my first year stateside ended, I wasn't so sure. Maybe the ones who died *were* the lucky ones. Though my body lived through that last night in Vietnam, I left a large part of my soul behind. At least those who died wouldn't have the memories, the nightmares, or the people spitting on them when they finally got home.

I'd imagined a glorified homecoming. Instead, I was abused. Nobody wanted to hear about my experiences in Vietnam; it seemed as though the entire country wanted to forget the whole sorry mess. Students were rioting, brothers were fighting and quarreling about the right and wrong of it; I felt caught in the middle.

I could not get the war off my mind. I kept seeing the same scenes over and over. People dying. The injured crying for help. Failure, with all its pain and fear, stood on me like a giant in lead boots. As a good soldier, I'd done what my country asked me to do. Now I was a social outcast for participating in an "unpopular" war. It felt like everyone I met blamed me for our involvement in Vietnam.

My country's disapproval took away any pride I felt in a job well done.

Eventually, I found my escape. I began to drink a lot of alcohol and take drugs. I couldn't control my behavior; but the alcohol and drugs gave me an acceptable excuse to behave and react in inappropriate ways. They helped me sleep without so many nightmares. They numbed my emotions. With drugs, I could make it through a day without breaking down and crying uncontrollably about the turn my life had taken.

The war hadn't ended for me; it only changed locations.

Now, almost forty years later, I am still fighting the war. Though now I concentrate on helping my combat brothers leave their war behind, I am still recouping the damage done by that experience. Like Jim, I have observed dozens—perhaps hundreds of veterans struggle with issues of isolation and intimacy.

I've watched men move from relationship to relationship, over and over again, never really identifying the cause of their failure. I've known women who tolerate veteran husbands who disappear for months at a time—completely unable to maintain the physical closeness of marriage and family. I've seen veterans retreat, rather than struggle to maintain a difficult relationship.

I've long wondered about these issues. Wondered about their causes. Wondered if injured people could change. And now, instead of wondering, I want to take action. I want to bring healing and wholeness to my combat brothers. I know that isolation racks all trauma survivors. Rape, domestic violence, assault, natural disaster—nearly any traumatic experience has the potential to keep us from the very ones who love us the most.

I know too that survivors **can** reconnect with people. We can trust others. We can learn the kinds of relational skills that make successful marriages and friendships. We can learn how to dismantle the crippling isolation which threatens our very existence. And in so doing, we can recoup the most valuable part of our humanity.

We can share our souls.

CHAPTER TWO

Why Try?

When two people connect being to being, they experience a deep "soul resonance" that goes beyond mere romance or desire. Something powerful and real inside them starts waking up and coming alive in each other's presence...

John Welwood, *Mothering*, Fall 1990

I can almost hear male readers groan, "Ah, man, not that soul stuff. Who needs it? Women are only trouble anyway."

Who needs relationships? We all do. Not only do humans need healthy male-female relationships, they need healthy friendships as well. In this book, we'll be focusing on healthy relationships of all kinds. Think of them as soul relationships— those kinds of connections between people characterized by honesty, trust, and mutual support.

Friendships—between men and women, husbands and wives— relationships with relatives, girlfriends—even employees and employers—any connection you wish to strengthen can benefit from the exercises I've included here.

At this point, you may be asking yourself: are healthy relationships even possible?

While it's true that relationships—be they friendships or marriages—can be difficult; at the same time, long-term, satisfying relationships have enormous potential. I can personally attest to the value of life-long friendships. My friends challenge me, support me, laugh at my humanity, and cry with my sorrows.

As for marriage, where else can men and women experience the most satisfying and enriching expression of our humanity and sexuality? There is no joy quite like having a fully committed life partner—one who knows everything there is to know about you and who chooses to love you anyway.

There is no relief like exposing your most cruel, or vile, or evil side and finding that you can be fully accepted and loved in spite of your weaknesses. Marriage, and for that matter committed friendship, can be a nearly divine interaction between two humans—divine because it mimics our Creator's relationship with us.

Divine? Absolutely. Your heavenly Father knows your every weakness and chooses to love you anyway.

Let me warn you; improving your human relationships will take work. Hard work.

I'll ask you to become aware—perhaps for the first time—of your own patterns of interaction. You'll be looking for emotions as you interact. Look especially for signs of anger, fear, avoidance, and isolation. As you reflect, I'll ask you to write things down.

Whether you chose to journal extensively or not, you'll want to make notes that remind you of the situations or behaviors triggered by the questions at the end of these chapters. Feel free to jot notes in the margins of these pages. Underline, circle, cross out. Do whatever you must to make the text fully your own.

Later, I'll ask you to begin making small changes in your relational style. You will gain the most if you start experimenting in safe, nonthreatening relationships. There, you can feel free to practice these skills, starting with the easiest changes first. Then, as you become more confident, you can try the skills in other settings with other people.

As you face your own behavioral patterns, you will experience many painful emotions. Your mind and feelings will try to convince you to give up. You may find yourself believing that you can't change. Don't let these messages stop your progress. Press on, in spite of the pain you experience. Freedom lies on the other side.

You may still be wondering why anyone would want to work at connecting. What difference does it make? What could possibly be wrong with living alone, keeping people away? After all, if connecting takes so much work, wouldn't it be easier and safer to leave things as they are?

Easier? Perhaps. Safer? Certainly. But rewarding? Fulfilling? Absolutely not!

Did you know that people in healthy relationships show overwhelming advantages in ways physical, social, financial, and psychological? In hundreds of studies researchers have found many benefits in those subjects with good connections:

- Married men are more likely to survive their first heart attack than unmarried men.[1]
- Both men and women in healthy relationships live longer. Single, divorced or widowed males have a mortality rate two to six times higher than their married peers.[2]
- Men and women in healthy relationships take fewer sick leaves than their single counterparts. As a marriage improves over time, both husband and wife report better health.[3]
- Married men are only half as likely as bachelors to take their own lives.[4]
- Healthy relationships provide a greater sense of satisfaction in life; research suggests that emotional well-being is highest in those who are continuously married.[5]

+ Healthy relationships measurably strengthen the immune system.[6]
+ Married cancer patients have a 15% greater survival rate than their single counterparts.[7]
+ Married men and women do better economically, more than twice the level of their single counterparts.[8]
+ Married men and women are less depressed, suicidal and prone to drug abuse than single, divorced, or widowed people of the same age.[9]

While researchers continue to document the positive benefits of healthy relationships, their work does not get to the heart of my concern—helping survivors and their partners strengthen ties to one another. With all my heart, I believe that men and women were created to connect.

All humans need nurturing, loving, and supportive relationships with others.

You may not choose to believe in Biblical truth. I won't try to change your mind. But I warned you earlier to expect my faith-based viewpoint. With that in mind, let me explain why I think humans were created for connection:

I find evidence for connection in the first three chapters of the Bible. In Genesis, God creates the world. He makes the earth and the sky and the seas and then proceeds to fill them with creatures. Over and over, he expresses his pleasure in his creation. "Man, that's good," he says (The Dean paraphrase). "Whoa, what a great job I did there!"

Then for his crowning achievement, God creates humankind—beginning with Adam. From the dust of the earth, he creates a man. Then he gives the man a garden and tells him to care for it. And then, as though he suddenly realizes his mistake, God says, "Whoops!"

Whoops?

What is it about this guy that distresses God so? Why does God express unhappiness with this particular aspect of creation? The man is alone.

Even though Adam had a perfect job tending the Garden of Eden and even though he lived in a perfect place and even though he spent time every single day with the God of the universe, it wasn't enough.

Man needed something more. He needed someone like himself. And so, God created woman. He brought her to the man and introduced them. And the man said, "Right on, God!"

From the beginning of creation, God saw our need for human interaction. Even before sin clouded the picture, God saw that humans needed other humans to help us find our way in life. After the first sin, our need for human interaction only grew. Having been thrown out of the Garden, and losing our face to face relationship with God, we need others to see us through the pain, the joy, and the frustration, the wonder, and difficulty of human existence. We shouldn't do it alone. We shouldn't try.

We weren't made to make it through life alone.

Whenever any human experiences the intense loneliness of my friend Jim, you can be certain that the dash light for loving human interaction will go off. "Take care of me," the soul cries. "Don't make me do this alone."

I like Alfred Ells' explanation in his book, *One Way Relationships* (Thomas Nelson, 1990). This is his concept, in a nutshell: Every human is born with certain undeniable needs— for affection (love expressed), for acceptance (of who we really are) for attention (that we matter), for affiliation (belonging), for approval (of our ability and personhood), and for affirmation (for our uniqueness among others).

In healthy families, parents meet these primary emotional needs in their children. Having our needs met, we grow up with a healthy sense of self. As we mature, we learn to carry our sense of love, acceptance, and approval inside ourselves, depending less and less on others to meet these needs.

However, as we mature these needs don't go away. Healthy adults continue to meet these basic human needs in the context of healthy human relationships.

These needs are *not* a sign of weakness. In fact, the need for human connection is no more a sign of weakness than your need for oxygen to keep your brain cells working or food to keep your muscles contracting.

Denying your need for others doesn't make it go away. In fact, denying your need may be the most successful way I know to be certain that the need will never be met. When we deny the need, we may actually amplify, rather than minimize it.

So what happens when humans interact in healthy relationships?

For one thing, we experience the deep satisfaction of being valuable, of being needed. We experience the intense joy of enhancing the life of someone we love by giving away a part of ourselves. Just as your fingerprint is completely distinct, and your voice cannot be perfectly recreated by any other human, so also is the unique contribution you make to the lives of those you love. No one does it like you.

Your friends, your wife, your loved ones, *need* you.

And *you need* your friends.

This is another critical value of connectedness: *Only as we interact in a real and meaningful way with other humans, can we begin to know ourselves.* We see our kindness, our compassion, our creativity, our wisdom reflected in our interaction with other humans. Only in close relationships do these valuable assets find their deepest expression.

All the best in us comes forth as we connect with others. Our ability to love someone through physical difficulty is tried and proven in the context of a committed relationship. In committed relationships, we discover our capacity for generosity, for gentleness, for forgiveness—because these things find expression when they are needed by those we love.

But another side comes forth as well. *Only in real connection with other humans are we confronted by our own capacity for evil.* We find it reflected in our unkindness, impatience, and unforgiveness. We hear it in the accusations, complaints, and in the frustrations our loved ones express over our repetitive and unproductive behaviors. Only in our relationships with others, do we face our need to grow and change.

When we hold others at arm's length, we give them no access to anything but what my mother used to call our "Sunday-best behavior." At arm's length, no one knows that I don't pick up my clothes, or that I have a short temper, or that I struggle with insecurity. I don't show my fears or my pride. In isolation I keep the truth about myself carefully under wrap. And kept under cover, my dark side never improves. Instead, it ferments and brings death.

I like this quote from John Welwood, in his article "Conscious Commitment:"

> The ground of a strong and lasting commitment is a passionate connection between two people whose beings say "yes" to each other. When two people connect being to being, they experience a deep "soul resonance" that goes beyond mere romance or desire. Something powerful and real inside them starts waking up and coming alive in each other's presence…Just as the body of a guitar amplifies and enriches the vibration of the strings to produce a full rich musical sound so does the resonance between two beings amplify and enrich the qualities of each one. This kind of soul connection is much more sustaining than personality…Out of this resonance grows a devotion to each other's well being. (*Mothering*, Fall 1990, 110)

So, here is my challenge:

Can you catch a glimpse of how meaningful relationships might benefit *your* life? One of my favorite stories is told by an adult who, as a severely handicapped child, was told he could never succeed. With stubborn determination, he overcame spastic cerebral palsy to learn to ride his own bike and play ball with his friends. In spite of a severe speech impediment, he entered the seminary. In the end, the child everyone expected to fail became a successful writer, pastor, and public speaker.

When he tells his story, this pastor repeats the theme of his life, expressed in this six-word tag line, "Ya got ta have the want-to."

If you have the "want-to"—if you have the desire to find and nourish healthy relationships—then this book is for you!

CHAPTER THREE

What's Normal, Anyway?

Dennis…has trouble concentrating, focusing his interests and committing to a career. Much of the time he feels like running, hoping a new environment will bring him some happiness, but it seldom does for long.

Dennis has gone through two divorces and two other close relationships with women have ended. "I have not been able to communicate feelings or relate on a day-to-day basis. I had nothing to give them; I felt worthless in relationships. These were spiritually good women, and they were there for me, but I couldn't be there for them. I had trouble being a stepfather because my wife's children reminded me of the children in Vietnam. I have done so much blocking out; there are so many things I have to work through."

Delores Kuenning, *Life After Vietnam*

L ike Dennis, you may be feeling a sense of hopelessness, wondering if you can ever have a meaningful relationship with anyone again. You may have divided your life into *Before the War* and *After the War*, or *Before the Rape* and *After the Rape*, believing that because of that one traumatic experience, you must live forever as an isolated individual, without anyone knowing who you really are, or caring about what you have suffered.

Not true. **People wounded by trauma can find and sustain meaningful relationships.**

Hopefully, by now you see the importance of emotional connections with the world around you. You've gotten a feel for the physical and psychological benefits of rewarding and connected relationships. Maybe, for the very first time, you've even considered the spiritual importance of human relationships.

Now, are you ready for a more personal question? Can you admit your own need for healthier connections?

You aren't alone in that need. In spite of the dismal divorce rates in our country, men and women still date. They continue to move in together. They still marry. Something inside drives us toward relationship. We yearn to connect with other human beings, no matter how hard it is to find that special person or how difficult the relationship is to maintain.

In the United States, more than half of all first marriages end in divorce. About 60 percent of second marriages fail. While this looks bad, the reality may actually be far worse. Of *recent* first marriages, the failure rate is nearer 60 percent.[1]

Keeping a healthy connection with another human is a difficult assignment for anyone.

But I believe survivors of severe trauma find the assignment especially formidable. Among Vietnam veterans for example, professional studies tend to focus on those who experience symptoms of Post-Traumatic Stress Disorder (PTSD). Clearly these studies and statistics reveal startling differences in the ability of veterans with PTSD to maintain intimate relationships. Veterans with PTSD:[2]

+ Are twice as likely as non-PTSD veterans to divorce.
+ Are three times as likely to divorce multiple times.
+ Report far less satisfaction with their intimate relationships and have equally dissatisfied partners.

Though few scientific studies have documented the relationship between PTSD symptoms and relationship quality, it takes little imagination to make the connection. Veterans and others wounded by trauma who struggle through life with PTSD exhibit severe emotional numbing, making it difficult for them to connect with their own feelings—let alone the feelings of their intimate partners.

At the same time, these survivors suffer from wild swings of anger and depression, rendering them either completely unavailable, or on the other hand, overtly dangerous. These unpredictable fits of rage can be terrifying to their partners. Even when they are not angry, survivors with PTSD tend toward aggressive and controlling behavior.

Both vets and trauma survivors may have difficulty obtaining or keeping employment. They may struggle with sleep disturbances, leaving them severely sleep deprived and terribly irritable. They tend to be hyper-vigilant, so determined to protect themselves from further injury that they become overly sensitive to others. Like sea anemone, they close up at the first sign of injury. Their communication skills deteriorate. Under stress, they avoid direct answers, or give unclear responses in an effort to deflect attention from their own issues.

In an effort to dull their own agony, many persons with PTSD abuse drugs and alcohol, clouding their ability to connect with and support friends and family. Already traumatized, addiction further damages their self-image, adding feelings of guilt and regret to deep anxiety and haunting memories.

Guilty people have difficulty being honest with others about their thoughts and feelings. In the end, they are even less able to work through difficult issues in connected relationships.

Left to themselves, persons wounded by trauma often lack hope.

Veterans with PTSD are not the only ones who suffer. Many veterans who have not been diagnosed also struggle with similar problems in their relationships. They too have difficulty with painful memories, with vulnerability, with openness, and with conflict resolution. In spite of this, they long for richer more fulfilling relationships.

What causes the struggle? Combat? Trauma? Military life?

The struggle may come from a combination of all those factors. In Vietnam, the average combat soldier was only 18.6 years old (much younger than his 23-year-old World War II counterpart).[3] At a time when his peers were attending college or vocational school, dating and moving out on their own, our soldiers found themselves embroiled in the life and death issues of combat.

Because they weren't at home, having normal young adult experiences, these veterans may have actually missed part of their normal developmental process. Having spent those crucial young adult years in the jungles of Southeast Asia, their emotional and psychological growth failed to follow its normal course.

All humans grow in phases. We see these most clearly in our physical development. Babies learn first to focus their eyes. Later, they hold up their heads. Eventually, they begin to crawl and later, learn to walk. We expect physical development to follow a predictable pattern. But babies also develop psychosocially—meaning that they learn psychological and social skills in similar predictable patterns.

Have you ever wondered why a two-month-old doesn't cry when his mother leaves the room? He isn't upset, because he does not yet understand that his mother still exists outside of his vision. For young babies, when he cannot see her, his mother simply ceases to exist. Psychologists call this concept Object Permanence.

Coincidentally, babies learn the concept of permanence at about the same time that they begin to display separation anxiety. You'll know when your son learns object permanence. There is no joy like the sudden hysteria of a nine-month-old when mommy leaves for work.

Different kinds of mental and psychological growth characterize *all* stages of human development. This growth doesn't end when your child starts school. Or, when your child graduates from high school. In fact, normal adults experience continued psychosocial development well into their twenties and thirties.

But in some cases, normal development stops. Children who suffer severe trauma (like the death of a parent, or a severe accident) may completely abandon normal progress. Others, for instance children who develop addictions, may suspend further maturity until they confront and break free of their addiction.

This explains why alcoholics who begin treatment in their late fifties often display the reasoning, confidence, and self-discipline of a teenager. Not only must they face their addiction; but as adults, they must work on unsolved developmental issues as well. These fifty-year-olds find themselves working on issues of personal responsibility, commitment, and self-denial.

In a similar way, the soldiers who served in Vietnam may have unfinished development as well. While their friends at home were exploring their first committed relationships, our soldiers learned to fire a weapon. While their friends had their first fights with girlfriends, our soldiers learned to kill or be killed. While their friends explored the benefits of intimacy, our soldiers learned to shut out the humanity of the guy beside them, hoping they might avoid the pain of watching him die.

Vietnam veterans missed many of the skills that normal humans learn over the course of their young adult years. And to make matters worse, when those men returned from the war, they found themselves with a full bag of new problems. New memories. New hurts. New complications. No veteran could pick up where he left off until he dealt with the problems he brought back from military service.

Now may be the time for you to pick up what you missed. It takes focused work. But things can improve. You can grow. And as you do, you will find yourself surrounded by deep, rewarding relationships that last a lifetime. At the same time, you will enhance the health and satisfaction of your marriage partner, your friends and your loved ones. These days, at a time when personal growth plans are widely popular, we can offer a plan that will benefit both you and the people you care about most.

So, assuming you want to change, where do you start?

Back in my old army days, during Weapons Training and Qualification, my instructor started us off shooting at targets. I didn't learn to shoot by pointing my weapon in the air and pulling the trigger. Instead, I had an objective, a pop-up silhouette that dropped away only after being struck by my bullet.

In the beginning, some of the guys I was with in boot camp looked like they were aiming for the sun. I don't think they'd ever held a gun before in their lives. With time, they learned to hit the target. Eventually, after hours on the range, all of us became proficient with our weapons.

The same is true in healthy, connected relationships. We need a target—a silhouette if you like that description. What does a good relationship look like? What makes them work? What skills do healthy partners bring to their relationships? How can people protect their relationships from the assaults of life in the twenty-first century?

What are the qualities of successful relationships—be they intimate, sexual relationships, or those flourishing relationships between committed friends? Can these qualities be named or quantified? And even if we could name them, don't these things *just happen* between people? Aren't relationships like that old Beach Boys' song: "Good Vibrations?"

Everyone knows you can't force good vibes. Or can you?

Absolutely. Starting today, you can begin to think of your friendships as individual high-yield savings accounts, where regular, planned deposits contribute to exponential long-term growth. You *can* force *good* vibrations by creating an environment where bad vibes don't flourish. It takes work, but it can be done.

> Two are better than one;
> Because they have a good return for their work.
> If one falls down, his friend can help him up.
> But pity the man who falls and has no one to help him up!
> Also, if two lie together, they will keep warm,
> But how can one keep warm alone?
> Though one may be overpowered,
> two can defend themselves.
> (Ecclesiastes 4:9-11 NIV)

So, what are the qualities of healthy relationships?

Before I list them, realize that these qualities are reciprocal. By this I mean that in healthy relationships, both persons have an equal responsibility to provide a healthy environment for one another. In healthy relationships, it is almost as if the partners agree to sign the following commitment in blood:

- **Trust.** I trust that you would never deliberately hurt me. In the same way, I promise I will never knowingly hurt you.
- **Acceptance.** I accept you just the way you are, even as you reveal yourself to me. I accept your point of view, and acknowledge it to be just as valid as my own.

+ **Identification.** I genuinely want to understand what it feels like to be you. I want to walk in your shoes.
+ **Vulnerability.** I want you to know the real me. As I can, because I trust your acceptance of me, I promise not to hide myself from you.
+ **Permanence.** No matter what we face, our relationship can survive. Even when I am disappointed, I will never abandon you or our relationship.
+ **Conflict Resolution.** When our desires conflict, I will work with you—not against you—to find a middle ground which is acceptable for both of us.
+ **Responsibility.** I am responsible for my own actions. I promise to acknowledge my errors and make a genuine effort to change whenever I can in order to strengthen our relationship.
+ **Guilt and Forgiveness.** When I mess up, I promise to admit it. I will ask for your forgiveness. To the best of my ability, I promise to forgive you in the same way I hope you will forgive me. I will leave my hurts behind as we move forward to strengthen our ties.

In each of the following chapters, we'll examine these commitments in more detail. We'll look at the ways our past—specifically the trauma in our past—interferes with our willingness and ability to exhibit these qualities. We'll try to find ways to change—small, safe ways at first—before we progress to scarier and more difficult skills. Stick with me. We can change. We can.

BUILDING BRIDGES

1. As you think back on your own childhood, did your parents have the kind of healthy relationship described in this chapter? What was missing?

2. Can you think of anyone you know with this kind of relationship? What one incident have you observed that illustrates their strength?

3. Do you believe that you might have this kind of relationship? Why? Why not?

4. Before you experienced trauma, did you have a close relationship, a close friendship? How did that relationship make you feel?

CHAPTER FOUR

Coping
with
Trauma

*He used to be sweet and interested in you and now he's
angry or indifferent.*
He used to have big plans, but now he does nothing.
*He watches TV like a zombie...He no longer enjoys his
hobbies.*
He doesn't like people. He doesn't want them around.
*He won't go to parties or restaurants, to the county fair. You
think he's a jerk,*
But he's screaming in his head, don't bunch up. You'll be
killed.

Patience Mason, *Recovering from the War*

Post-Traumatic Stress Disorder. Though we gained little
else from the war in Vietnam, we owe most of our understanding of Post-Traumatic Stress Disorder (PTSD) to the survivors of that bloody conflict. Without their experiences, and the
record of the profound struggle they faced as they returned

home, we would have almost no understanding of the remarkable ability of the human spirit to cope with intensely traumatic events.

PTSD is a completely normal human response to a profoundly abnormal event.

Because of the Vietnam veterans, we understand why survivors of the World Trade Center bombing struggle with their emotions months after escaping the buildings. We understand why they complain of flashbacks, insomnia, and depression. We know why the men of New York City's Engine Company 7 have lost the joy of the work they do. We know why survivors of rape need help resuming a normal life.

Without the veterans of Vietnam, we would have little to offer others who have undergone traumatic, life-changing experiences. All survivors of incest, crime, physical abuse, dysfunctional families, torture, concentration camps, flood, fire, or other natural disasters may at some point face symptoms of PTSD. Without the veterans, experts would have little to offer.

We must remember that persons with PTSD are *not* mentally ill. In fact, for the most part they are psychologically speaking, completely normal. PTSD is the psychological pattern that helps people cope after having survived a profoundly abnormal trauma.

Today, though many people are aware of PSTD, few have considered the specific ways that PTSD may actually frustrate the hopes of survivors to have normal healthy relationships with others.

How do you know if you or someone you love suffers from PTSD?

You begin by looking for a cluster of symptoms which may include any of the following: intrusive thoughts, sleep disturbances, flashbacks (or intrusive memories), nightmares, night sweats, emotional numbing (the inability to respond emotionally to others), survivor guilt, anxiety and over active startle reactions, inability to concentrate, depression, and sexual dysfunction. In survivors, each of these symptoms can take on a wide variety of appearances.

In some, the syndrome appears immediately after the traumatic event. Or, as in the case of many war veterans, the symptoms may lie dormant, only to crop up years, even decades later. Many people think of the 'Nam vet as a stereotype: a guy living on the street in a field jacket, packing a big knife, drunk, drugged, and crazy. How unfair!

Thousands of vets are professionals, well-educated, highly-paid, white-collar workers with fine families and influential friends. But even these highly functional veterans may have been "stuffing" the Vietnam experience inside for decades. The sudden onset of delayed symptoms can be triggered by a current trauma—the loss of a loved one, or of a job, the onset of physical illness, or even some relatively small bump in the everyday life of the survivor.

We do know that the development of PTSD depends on a variety of factors:

+ The severity of the trauma itself (in Vietnam, exposure to mutilation and death). Those who experienced more severe trauma are more likely to suffer with post-traumatic stress.
+ The duration of the stress (for combat veterans, a full year).
+ How the person sees the events in relation to himself (for some veterans, believing that the government has taken advantage of and then discarded them may increase their stress response).
+ The ability of the survivor to talk to someone about the events (Vietnam vets faced a nation full of people who didn't want to know what they experienced).
+ The reaction of others to what the survivor tells them (some veterans had no one who would listen or care. Others faced ridicule, or crass insults, or even rejection).

- Circumstances or luck (some survivors found someone who loved them. In spite of their trauma, they obtained meaningful employment, or developed a strong group of genuine friendships to help them through).

This explains why some veterans refer to those suffering with PTSD as whiners. Though they both fought in the same war, their experiences may have been vastly different—both in Vietnam and after returning to the United States. Both experiences—in war and at home—play an important part in the development of PTSD.

Persons who suffer from PTSD may exhibit only part of the collection of symptoms. Still, having any of these symptoms will affect your ability to find and maintain healthy relationships. The presence of these symptoms may be your wake-up call. There is help for PTSD—but only if you are willing to go after it.

You may wonder how something from the past can affect your present.

I think the best way to illustrate how PTSD affects our relationships is to refer to the chapter I wrote for veterans and veteran's families in the book *Nam Vet: Making Peace with Your Past*:

> Vietnam veterans are not the only victims of the war. Our families likewise suffer from the effects of PTSD. The emotional numbing, depression, and alienation that have isolated the veteran from his family are symptoms of his Post-Traumatic Stress from the war. The veteran's symptoms are usually obvious. But the psychological wounds within the family are not as readily perceived. Research clearly indicates that veteran families are affected both emotionally and spiritually by the veteran's stress…The world around us may think we have no problems, and most people would guess we were never in 'Nam. But

many of us display little quirks around our families that give us away. We are a bit fanatical about cleanliness, order, and especially security. If we come home late and find the house unlocked, we throw a tantrum that borders on panic. Our family suffers, walking on eggshells, never knowing when we may fly off the handle completely (even though we've never done it, they feel we may at any time). They live on the edge of *something* they can't explain.

Some of us never realize that PTSD lies at the root of our problems. We live in a private hell. We secretly struggle to find resolution for our traumatic experiences—be they war or rape. Facing constant but intangible pressure from the past, we use our families as the unfortunate targets of our stress. In fact, *each* of the symptoms of PTSD adds another obstacle to finding and maintaining healthy relationships.

Intrusive Thoughts.

Psychologist John Wilson believes that traumatic events need to be assimilated and integrated by the person who experiences them. In everyday terms—the horror and terror eventually become part of the fabric of survivor. Until this happens, the psyche continues to hold the event in active memory stage, where those memories periodically emerge as unsettling or emotionally disturbing images of the event.

This explanation of intrusive thoughts gives little comfort to those who struggle with them. Try as he might, the survivor cannot keep these images from reappearing. He cannot control the timing or the effect of their appearance. How can a Trade Center survivor focus on Johnny's lunch money or picking up the kids, when brutal images of falling bodies repeatedly explode into his thoughts? How can a survivor of rape enjoy a romantic comedy when all she sees on the screen of her mind is the mocking smile of her attacker?

As intrusive thoughts continue to batter away at the survivor's consciousness, he has trouble staying in the here and now. His attention is being drawn away by the memories, leaving him little enthusiasm for the present. Unable to exist solely in the present, the survivor's partner feels cheated—as though she is competing with a ghost she cannot see.

Sleep Disturbances

As intrusive thoughts steal the survivor's emotional energy, nightmares, sleep disturbances, and night sweats combine to drain the survivor's physical energy. Psychologists know that prolonged sleep deprivation can cause full-blown psychosis in normal human adults. How much more damage can thirty years of interrupted sleep create for the veterans of the Vietnam War?

When a survivor struggles with perpetual fatigue, he also struggles in all areas of normal function. His ability to listen, to empathize, to reason are all diminished by pervasive and unrelenting fatigue. His temper may be short. His attention may be diminished. His coordination is affected. All of this may not be a direct result of the trauma itself but an indirect result of the body's attempt to cope with the trauma.

Emotional Numbing

The soldier in the field becomes an expert at shutting down his emotions. The veteran, who held his best friend during the last shudders of death, immediately picked up his rifle and went on with his own work. He has experienced the ineptitude of the military the frustration of fatal mistakes, the loss of many comrades, and fallen instantly asleep in an earthen hole. He woke up the next day, ate his rations, and moved out. I wrote this about emotional numbing in my *Nam Vet* book:

> In 'Nam, we learned that to get close to anyone was to ask
> for trouble. We were emotionally vulnerable to pain when

we developed close relationships, and the chances were great that any relationship would end suddenly in an ambush or booby trap. One moment I could be standing there talking to a friend, and the next I'm wearing his brains on the front of my shirt. In order to maintain any control of sanity, we had to freeze our senses. When we wanted to scream or strike out at someone or something for causing us to lose our closest friend, we couldn't. There was no answer except to make us "hard core" to anything emotional or sensitive. It didn't even do any good to cry.

The survivor's expertise at numbing is so precise that the soldiers of Vietnam developed a phrase to express it. "Don't mean nothin'," was their way of numbing the deep frustration of fighting a war no one would ever win.

This kind of numbing effectively shuts down a wide variety of emotions. Some veterans use all their energy to control a rage that roars like a spring-melt river through their psyche. Afraid of hurting others, or of unleashing a monster they cannot control, they spend enormous amounts of energy keeping it all tucked under the surface of their everyday lives.

Others, afraid of unleashing the intense grief of severe loss, use emotional numbing to keep the pain away. These veterans have lost friends, some have lost their health, their youth, their faith, their families, their trust in the government—even their belief in right and wrong. They fear letting go of their emotions, wondering if the grief might kill them.

Some vets are convinced that they have lost their personhood—the person who went to war never came home. They believe they have no hope for a happy life. These losses boil inside of them like a cauldron of acid. Afraid of the damage such grief might cause, the survivor is desperate to keep it under control. Unfortunately, in order to keep his anguish under cover, he must reject all feelings, even the ones connected to the here and now.

Having numbed these dangerous emotions, the survivor is left without the ability to feel even the best of emotions. He no longer laughs or finds pleasure in ordinary life. He may even have avoided sexual intimacy—afraid that those moments of intense pleasure might unleash emotions he cannot control.

Emotional numbing has an unintended effect on families as well. As they watch the survivor isolating himself and numbing his emotions, they begin to believe that this is the way life is supposed to be lived. The wife forgets how to laugh. The children grow up afraid of making any loud or sudden noises, losing a natural childhood to the cold isolation the survivor brings into the home.

Anticipating unpredictable responses, families begin to cover their own emotions. Children of survivors may even begin to avoid intimate contact because they quickly learn that they invariably get hurt when they get close to someone they love.

HYPER VIGILANCE

As the survivor overreacts to environmental triggers—like crushing pop cans, backfiring cars, or the sound of a helicopter—with bizarre self-protective behavior, they often frighten and confuse their loved ones. Their over-reaction can turn an ordinary moment into a crisis. Many times their reaction manifests as hostility. Since they are usually closest, wives and children become prime targets for this hostility.

I know of one wife who learned not ever to touch her husband while he slept. Once, she had rolled over in bed, touching him. He woke instantly, and had her in a choke hold before he recognized his mistake. The event badly frightened both of them.

Though the survivor's response kept him alive in the face of a real threat, it looks out of place in downtown Portland or Seattle. He/she feels embarrassed about their behavior and sorry to have embarrassed their loved ones. Sometimes the survivor withdraws from relationships to make certain it never happens again. The thinking may go like this, *If we aren't together when I respond to a trigger, then I won't feel ashamed to have you see me dive under a table, or punch out a stranger.*

The symptoms of PTSD interfere with the survivor's ability to cope with the normal stresses of everyday life. The survivor—in an effort to control his own symptoms—ends up trying to control other people: his wife, his children, his coworkers, and his friends. None of these coping mechanisms really rid the survivor of his symptoms.

The best thing any survivor can do is to stop the pattern. There are numbers of qualified professionals who can help. Medications may be temporarily helpful for insomnia and depression, but they are not long-term cures. For most survivors who work at it, with time and therapy medications become unnecessary.

The partners of survivors should remember one thing: these symptoms are not about you. Nothing you do or don't do can ever cure your partner. While that fact may make you feel hopeless, at the same time, it absolves you of the responsibility to fix your partner. You can't. You can't make him get help. You can't become his therapist.

But you can try to understand what he may be going through. Read all you can about PTSD. Become informed. Be available to your partner. You can help create an environment where your partner decides to seek help for himself.

You can both decide not to let Post-Traumatic Stress Disorder rob you of your most precious relationships.

BUILDING BRIDGES

1. Have you experienced difficulty sleeping? Getting to sleep? Staying asleep?
2. Do you have a nightmare that recurs frequently? Do you remember the nightmare? Can you associate the dream with some event in your past?

3. Have you found yourself using drugs or alcohol to get away from memories that seem to be with you all the time?

4. Do sounds and smells have the power to take you back in time to some traumatic event?

5. Do you find it difficult to care about or attend to the issues of your daily life?

6. When was the last time you cried? What made you cry? How did you feel about letting the sorrow out?

7. Have you found yourself unable to feel something you know you ought to feel? Like grief at the death of a loved one?

8. How about laughter? Do you have difficulty finding or expressing humor?

9. If you are having trouble expressing emotions, which emotion do you miss the most?

CHAPTER FIVE

Relationships and Memories— Rules of Engagement

It's hard to tell someone what it smells like when a mine goes off and the smell of gunpowder and flesh is mixing in the air...[1]

Ken Hodges, My Lai witness

Maintaining a healthy relationship is hard enough without the added effects of post-traumatic stress. By distracting its victims, PTSD steals energy, leaving survivors numb and unfocused, sometimes even completely overwhelmed. Often those who suffer from PTSD find themselves unable to remove the past from their present. All the while, the injured struggle to cope with the normal stresses of everyday life.

While the effects of PTSD may never be completely erased, the disorder can be disarmed. I picture PTSD as a minefield covered with hidden dangers and explosions. This kind of danger can be ignored—left to cause severe damage in some unexpected blast, or skilled engineers can clear the minefield. Though the task is difficult, clearing the ground of explosives is the only way for survivors to move forward safely.

We must find and disarm these dangerous memories.

We do it by allowing ourselves to remember the painful events fully, bringing them out into the open. As we remember, we focus on the truth about what happened, rejecting bits of untruth (even those we have believed for long periods), and accepting what happened as part of who we are—our personal experience.

This process is what Dr. Wilson meant by integration—weaving our memories of trauma into the fabric of our life. In the process, the memories are disarmed—rendered powerless to destroy our present well-being.

Some survivors require professional help in this daunting task. This is especially true for those whose closest relationships (professionals call these relationships the survivor's "support system") are neither intimate enough nor strong enough to stand the additional strain of sorting through the past. For others, professional help may not be necessary. These survivors find healing in the loving care of healthy, close relationships.

In other words, if a survivor with PTSD has managed to establish and maintain healthy relationships (sometimes this is because his loved ones refuse to let him disconnect), he will thrive in those relationships and find healing. If the survivor has few safe relationships, then the outside help of a professional counselor can provide much needed support and expertise.

Before you start work on issues of PTSD, it may help if you and your partner (or friend) begin by talking about relationships in general. Ask one another about past relationships—especially those that felt safe. What made them feel that way? Could you talk about anything? Did you feel that the other person accepted your ideas? What things did the safe person do or say that made you feel listened to and understood?

What about bad relationships? What people or situations have hampered your ability to talk openly in less comfortable relationships? Did that person refuse to let you talk? Did he say so? How did you know that he didn't want to listen? What made it a bad relationship? Did you feel judged?

Talk about truth. Why is truth important in relationships? What might the two of you do to encourage truth-telling in your relationship? Are you both committed to the truth?

What about acceptance? What does acceptance mean? Why is it important? What can someone do to help you feel accepted?

By exploring these ideas together, you may gain some clues as to how to encourage more intimate conversation between the two of you. Perhaps she wants to hold hands while she talks. Perhaps he needs to have her look at him in order to know that she is listening. Perhaps she hates being interrupted, or he needs to talk while doing something active—like walking or driving. Whatever you learn, apply your knowledge as you begin to explore the past together.

TALKING AND LISTENING

When the past demands our attention, as it does in flash-backs and nightmares, it is best to respond. By now, most of us have already discovered the ineffectiveness of well-meaning suggestions like, "Forget about it. Just put it behind you."

Survivors understand that these kinds of words of others may actually intensify their struggle.

Through flashbacks and nightmares, the soul is begging for help. No amount of self-medication, or stuffing, will put the past in its place. Instead, the best course of action is to respond. Like a child with a fever, the most effective approach is to address the cause of the fever while at the same time working to ease the symptoms.

So, commit yourselves to talking through the symptoms. When painful memories intrude, decide to face them head on.

Sometimes the intrusion will come in the form of a trigger—a frightening sound or a familiar smell—followed by some bizarre and seemingly inappropriate reaction. I know soldiers who have identified backfiring cars and Asian food as triggers for painful memories. Already, survivors of the Trade Center attacks are reporting flashbacks occurring at the sound of emergency sirens.

Whatever the trigger, only you can choose to disarm it.

Begin by finding a safe time and place to talk about your memory of the incident with someone you trust. Recall as many of the details as you possibly can. Think about what you smelled, what you heard, what people around you said and did. Share those details with your partner. If it becomes too much to talk about in one session, agree to talk again later. But tell as much as you can.

And then go further.

Try to recall the feelings you had at the time of the incident. Put words on the feelings—words like frightened, confused, angry or hopeless. Explore why you might have felt the way you did. Let yourself feel those feelings again, even the most painful of them. Look carefully for feelings of sadness, or helplessness.

If you are the listening partner, do your best to listen actively. Acknowledge the details you are hearing. Express empathy for what your partner has experienced. Try to feel the event as your partner felt it, with all the fear and anger and vulnerability he may have felt.

Express your empathy. "That must have been frightening," or "I can see why you would feel so angry." Try not to judge the responses of the survivor. Don't feel that you must hide your own reaction to the words you hear. Sometimes, your reaction can verify the very emotion the survivor felt but may be afraid to express.

During these conversations, the survivor may feel things he has never allowed himself to feel before. He may need to grieve for those who did not survive. He may find his anger toward some irresponsible authority suddenly surface. Let your survivor feel it—whatever emotion arises in the process. Be prepared to love and accept him through those emotions.

Be careful about your own response to what you hear. The story may be so traumatic as to make you physically uncomfortable. Don't let your body language tell your partner that you don't want to listen. Maintain eye contact. Touch your partner. Hold his hand or put an arm around his shoulder if this seems appropriate. Accept what you hear no matter how difficult or uncomfortable the truth may make you feel. Let yourself cry if you feel like it.

If your partner seems willing, ask questions. Be careful not to let your questions interrupt the narrative flow. Remember how difficult it is for your partner to confront his past. Don't let interruptions provide an excuse to quit before making progress. If your questions seem to block the flow, save them for later.

Avoid analyzing your partner's memories. Glib comments, like "You did the best you could," or "It wasn't your fault; after all, you did what you were told," can actually impede the process. Hearing these words may make it harder for your partner to tell you the whole story. Try not to evaluate as you listen.

Often with trauma, memories become distorted. One traumatic incident can become a many-stranded cord that ties us to our past. In most cases, none of the strands have names. Instead, vague occurences bind them together to form an unrelenting misery that keeps us from moving forward.

With careful listening and gentle questions, you can help your partner recognize and reject the distortions left by trauma. Finding the truth together can release any barriers that might block the healing process.

Let me give an example: Suppose your survivor feels guilty that he didn't do more to save the lives of others. Firefighters who managed to escape the World Trade Center before its collapse, struggle with feelings that they should have done more to get their fellow firemen out of the building—out of harm's way.

Ask the survivor what he thinks he might have done. Ask if his idea might really have been possible. Did he know enough to make a difference? (For instance, at the time of the terror attacks on the World Trade Center, the fire fighters inside Tower One had no idea that Tower Two had been hit by another airplane. When the second tower fell, the men inside Tower One did not know the building next door had collapsed. Even when the orders were given to evacuate the building, these men had no idea that the Pentagon had been hit, or that a plane had gone down in Pennsylvania. In the midst of the evacuation, they functioned with almost no understanding of the very events in which they participated.)

Did your survivor have the time to make a difference? Did he have the authority? If he had been able to change specific events, would those changes have affected the overall outcome?

As you ask questions, let your survivor recognize the reality of the circumstances without your insistence. With time, his distortions will settle out, leaving a more balanced truth in its place.

Sometimes, dealing with the past brings up areas of personal responsibility and failure. Your partner may have contributed in some way to the painful memories. Let your partner analyze his contribution. If he should determine that he was responsible, allow him to accept responsibility and seek forgiveness.

Your expression of forgiveness may be just what your partner needs to hear.

I read of a medic who came upon a downed United States fighter plane in a Vietnam rice paddy. The injured pilot had survived the crash, but could not get himself out of the plane. The plane had caught fire, and the medic could not get through the flames to save the pilot. Desperate, the medic had emptied his handgun into the cockpit—his bullets ending the pilot's screaming cries of anguish.

For thirty years, the medic had nightmares. For the rest of his life, he saw the pilot's accusing eyes. He could not escape the truth. He had murdered the pilot.

No well-articulated platitudes could ease the medic's discomfort. Only full forgiveness can ease his pain. Fortunately, forgiveness is possible; we'll cover this in more detail later.

When you help your survivor to name the strands that bind him to his past, you enable your partner to let go of his mistakes, and to cut loose those ties he had no power over. Name them. Fear. Inexperience. Drunkenness. Selfishness. Mistakes. Whatever they are, separating and identifying them are the first steps toward cutting the ties that bind us to our past.

SPACE AND TIME

Not long ago, I went to a biking seminar designed to help riders train for century rides—the name given to one hundred mile rides completed in one day. Our speaker explained that the most often overlooked training ingredient was rest. "Progress must follow a three steps forward, one step backward pattern," he said. "It isn't optional. Without it, burnout will disrupt the training schedule."

He wanted us to see the pattern (increasing mileage every week for three weeks, followed by a low mileage week) as a *benefit* to training, not a setback. The body needs time to recuperate from the hard work of riding and strength building.

And so does the soul.

So when your partner seems to pull back and put up walls, let him. It may be that his soul needs a break. You can give him the space he needs by letting him pull away safely. He may need only a day or two to recover. Or, he may require more time.

I remember confronting painful issues in my own past. At times, the process seemed to cast a terrible shadow over my present. I wondered if I would ever laugh again. At times, I ran from the process, canceling appointments with my therapist and driving aimlessly for miles as my soul wallowed in pain. Today, I realize how much energy the healing process demands. I don't feel badly about taking time out.

When your partner pulls back, give him the room he needs. Reassure him of your commitment. Let him know that you'll be around to listen whenever he needs it. By giving permission to pull back, you enable your partner to try again at some time in the future, knowing that he can trust you not to push him beyond his ability.

Your gift of time and space are valuable contributions to your partner's healing process. He may need to be physically distant for some time. When he realizes that you care deeply for him, and that his experiences and emotions are always safe with you, he'll come back. Don't worry. Let go of the leash.

Professional Help

Sometimes, no amount of listening can untangle the web of trauma we've experienced in our lives. We talk and listen and still our destructive coping behaviors continue. Perhaps the lure of alcohol or drugs is more than we can resist. Or, perhaps our anger has become a pattern—a threat to the health and safety of those we love. When these things happen, it may be time to get professional help.

Back in the old days, when Vietnam veterans first returned from combat, few people understood the damage trauma inflicted on the human psyche. Many veterans never found competent professional help. Today though, I can tell you with confidence that many experienced professionals are available to help you face and disarm the damage of your past. With their help, you can change your life.

Of course you must begin the process. You must find someone you trust and make that first appointment. It is difficult. But in the long run, maintaining the self-destructive pattern is *much* more painful.

If your partner needs more help than you can give him, suggest that he find professional help. Offer to take him to the first appointment. But like the old horse and water, you can't make him go. That decision must remain with the survivor.

As the partner of a survivor, your only choice is to get help for yourself. You might try a support group—one specifically geared toward the trouble you face—toward partners of alcoholics or drug abusers or for domestic violence. This may be enough. Or you may need to begin your own counseling process. There you may find the strength and wisdom you need to maintain yourself in the face of your partner's traumatic past.

Sometimes, your decision to get help is just what your partner needs. By facing your own struggles, your partner may gain courage to battle with his past.

At the very least, you will find ways to disengage your emotions from your partner's struggle. You don't have to cycle through your partner's ups and downs. By getting help, you will be a better partner, a stronger person, and when children are present, a much better, more protective parent. These choices will help you no matter what choice your partner makes for his or her own future.

When both partners commit to the process, a loving relationship can be rich ground for healing and release. While you can't be responsible for your partner's choices, you can make your own.

You can choose to grow and heal.

BUILDING BRIDGES

1. In your present life, who really seems to want a relationship with you? Would that person listen if you wanted to talk through the issues discussed in this chapter?
2. What has that person done to earn your trust?
3. Can you think of one specific memory related to the trauma that you would erase if you could? Why do you think that memory came to mind first? Is it the most painful?
4. What might be the worst thing that could happen if you shared your memories with someone you trust? What

might be the best thing that could happen, if you talked through your memories?

5. If you can't quite begin, could you talk to that person about your desire to begin working through the memories?

6. If you have no one in your life now, would you consider the possibility of professional help?

7. Might someone help you find a counselor at a price you can afford? What might you be willing to give up in order to budget for professional help?

8. Make a list of all the things that keep you from beginning the process. Every day for as long as it takes, do something that will remove one item from the list.

9. When you have crossed the last item off the list, call your friend for coffee or make the appointment with someone who can help you.

CHAPTER SIX

Why Can't
I Trust You?

*My marriage is falling apart. We just don't talk any more. I
guess we've never really talked about anything—ever. I
spend most of my time at home alone in the basement. She's
upstairs and I'm downstairs. Sure, we'll talk about the groceries and who will get gas for the car, but that's about it.
She's tried to tell me that she cares for me, but I get real
uncomfortable talking about things like that, and I get up
and leave. Sometimes I spend more time on the road just
driving aimlessly than I do at home.*

A Disabled Combat Veteran

Living alone in the midst of a relationship—two people
with a continent between them, living in the same house.
How does that happen? Certainly people don't get married to
be alone. What is it about trauma that makes its victims more
likely to choose isolation over intimacy? Loneliness over com-
panionship?

And what is intimacy, anyway? How can we aim for a target we don't understand?

I believe that most humans live two lives.

In our outer lives, we project to others only those qualities we want them to see. We may let them believe we are strong and independent, or confident and carefree. Because our outer lives tend to be characterized by *good* qualities, we freely expose those qualities we like about ourselves—our sense of humor, our creativity, our dependability.

But we all have an inner life as well. In this life we tend to hide our less desirable selves. Because we perceive this inner life to be made up of *bad* characteristics, we protect others from this side of our personality. Here, in our deepest places, we hide our fears, our insecurities, our painful experiences, and our mistakes. These are the feelings and experiences we reveal only when we feel completely safe.

For our purposes then, healthy intimacy describes a relationship where two persons feel such unfailing security in their relationship to one another, that they can fully reveal both their inner and outer selves. In an intimate relationship, we know that our partner will affirm our strong qualities. But more than that, we also have confidence that our partner will accept us as we reveal our weaknesses.

In fact, over time we experience complete acceptance in a healthy intimate relationship. We know that our partner accepts both our strengths **and** our weaknesses. In an intimate relationship, the whole person is nurtured by his partner in a context of genuine concern for his well-being. In one sentence, we could define intimacy this way:

> Intimacy is the willingness to reveal all aspects of ourselves to our intimate partner, knowing that our strengths, our skills, our fears, and our faults, will all be equally accepted by the one we trust.

TRUST AND VULNERABILITY

I believe these are two sides of the same coin. Only in the context of trust can vulnerability exist. When we are confident of our safety, we can choose to bring out the parts of us that seem bad or difficult or painful. Only in the context of love can we finally confront and destroy the demons which haunt our inner man.

But wouldn't it be easier to hide behind the walls we build?

What is so important about trust and vulnerability? Why aren't we satisfied by conversations about the groceries and the car keys? Lori Gordon, (*Psychology Today*, September 1993, Vol. 26, Number 5) expresses the effects of an isolated relationship this way:

> Confusion. Hurt. Silence. Missed Opportunity. It is one of the ironies of modern life that many couples today are living together as complete strangers. Or worse, in great unhappiness.

What makes us unhappy living life alone? Why do we long to reach out toward other human beings? Psychologist and family specialist Dr. James Dobson answers that question in his book *What Wives Wish Their Husbands Knew about Women*: (Tyndale House, 1975):

> Self-esteem is only generated by what we see reflected about ourselves in the eyes of other people. It is only when others respect us that we respect ourselves. It is only when others love us that we love ourselves. It is only when others find us pleasant and desirable and worthy that we come to terms with our own egos...The vast majority of us are dependent on our associates for emotional sustenance each day. What does this say, then, about those who exist in a state of perpetual isolation, being deprived of loving caring human contact year after year? Such people are virtually

certain to experience feelings of worthlessness and its stepchildren, deep depression and despair. (Page 60)

Though intimacy is a worthy goal, all humans struggle to obtain it. While we long to be fully known, at the same time, we are terrified of rejection. We all recognize the face of rejection, from the subtle clues in posture or facial expression to the outright rejection of words or separation. As we are, we believe we are truly unlovable. The fear of rejection can wrap humans in a cocoon of isolation.

BETRAYED

Though all humans struggle with intimacy, survivors of trauma have a particularly difficult assignment. For them, an experience over which they had no control has shattered their trust in other humans. In many cases, the trauma itself marked only the beginning of the damage. Many survivors have also experienced secondary hurts inflicted by those they believed would protect them. Survivors sometimes feel blamed by their loved ones—as though perhaps something the survivor did contributed to the trauma they experienced.

How many rape victims are accused of "asking for the assault" because of their dress or behavior? How many are treated badly by police detectives, emergency room physicians, or defense attorneys? How many victims of theft are blamed for their negligence?

And how many Vietnam veterans have been blamed for their participation in an immoral war? How many came home to cries of "baby killer" screamed by war protestors? In her book, *Recovering from the War*, Patience Mason tells this story, "Another vet who was pulled out of a pile of dead bodies at Khe Sanh and came home critically wounded, remembered being spat on by protesters as he lay on the litter." This kind of secondary trauma compounds the enormous emotional injury inflicted by the war itself.

Once betrayed, trust is difficult to rebuild.

Broken trust has another dangerous quality. Like water damage in subflooring, the dry rot of trauma begins to seep into other areas of our lives. Even though our injury came from one place, victims try desperately to protect themselves from further injury inflicted by unrelated sources. Having experienced injury followed by betrayal, survivors begin to assume that no one can be trusted and posture themselves for safety even before danger appears.

For those whose trust has been betrayed, their intimate relationships suffer as well. They begin to question the safety of all relationships, wondering if they can ever reveal their inner struggles to anyone. It is as if they wonder *will this person hurt me too?*

Of course, when the one we love has truly hurt us, the injury must be addressed. But for survivors of trauma, our issues of mistrust tend to be displaced—that is, *left over* from other hurts inflicted in our past. Overcoming our own suspicion and mistrust is a matter of choosing to trust again and beginning, bit by bit, to open up in a safe relationship.

Afraid of Loss

In the seventies, the rock group Ten Years After had a song titled, "I Don't Know You Don't Know My Name." It was kind of a dumb name for a song, but I always liked it. Today, the song makes a lot more sense.

As I write, it happens to be the Christmas season, and I have waited as long as I possibly can to do any shopping. Why? Because like most veterans, I hate crowds. I get major jitters and anxious in places like department stores and shopping malls. But today after church, I bucked up and ventured out to a nearby mall.

I planned to search, seize, and withdraw as quickly as possible. As I headed out of the mall (at double-time, I might add), with the day's mission accomplished, I spotted a couple of guys wearing black baseball caps.

Even in the swarm, I recognized the words "Vietnam Veteran" in big gold letters across the front of their hats. I stopped them and said, "Welcome home"—which is my usual greeting. We exchanged combat details and had a good old time of greeting, handshaking, laughing, and hugging (all of which lasted about five minutes). Soon, we waved and took off in different directions.

It felt good running across them that way. It was nice to meet a "brother" while being "malled." However, as I walked to my car, I realized that our meeting dramatized something left over from our war experiences. We had just acted out what had been sub-consciously ingrained into us while serving in Vietnam.

Not once in our encounter did these men volunteer their names, nor did I share mine.

We had followed the unwritten rule of the Vietnam jungle. Never exchange real names.

To this day, I can remember the real and complete names of only a couple of the guys I served with. Instead, we used nick-names. These I remember even today, along with my buddies' physical appearances and what they did.

Why did soldiers fighting in Vietnam adopt this strange form of anonymity?

We did it to preserve our hearts. If we knew a fellow soldier's name, we somehow knew them as a person, a real person. Knowing too much personal information about one another seemed to increase the risk of forming soul-attachments—attachments that tore our souls apart when someone we knew died.

To know a fellow soldier's name, his hometown, his sisters, and brothers, his kids, and his wife made him too human to handle. When we put him in a body bag, we needed to be able to say, "Hey, 'Ace' got wasted. Get a dust-off in here for the body...okay let's move out!"

We could not afford to imagine that "Ace" had a girlfriend. A real person back home who wrote to him and called him Clyde. A girlfriend who one day hoped to be "Mrs. Clyde

Jones," daughter-in-law of Mr. and Mrs. James Jones who lived in Pleasantville, Ohio.

No, "Ace" was just "Ace"—a damn good machine gunner. Now that he was dead, that's all we wanted to remember about him.

Soldiers followed the rule about real names so that we could remain strong enough to get up and fight another day in a war cloaked in many uncertainties. Using nicknames helped us maintain the necessary distance to avoid being hurt by losing someone close to us.

So how does this safe distance behavior affect our relationships at home?

When we returned from Vietnam, we brought a duffel bag of clothes and other personal items. But we had more than that with us—we carried things you couldn't see. We brought home pieces of our lives we wanted to leave in Vietnam but couldn't. We brought home a collection of oaths and decisions we made while under the stress of war. While these oaths kept us alive over there, they inadvertently became a part of our civilian life. One of those oaths—the unwillingness to know others as individual human beings—came home with us as well.

We came home determined to avoid genuine attachments with other humans.

Because of our resolution (refusing to form attachments), we never get deeper than the first layer of relationship—everything stays on the surface. We continue to avoid the threat of going deep. This excerpt from Charlie, a Vietnam veteran illustrates how the principle works in real life:

> Me and my new friends, when we were in the rear in a relative safe area, would sit in our spot and just talk. Talk about girls, cars, home and anything but combat. It was fun and it had a sort of release from the stress of combat...We never talked about death or war during those times...just happy things.

...After a major operation, my friends and me wandered over to our spot and started talking like we usually did. But something was different this time. Now I found out why people didn't get close in Nam, as I looked around, there was one less person. Then the next time we got a chance to go to our spot, there was one less and so on.

It made us distant, not wanting to be too close to anyone so if someone died it didn't hurt so much. We had a phrase there we'd use, "Don't mean nothin'." Oh it meant a lot, but we would tell ourselves it didn't mean anything when something happened. But it always hurt the same. Back in the States, when I got home, this distance was so ingrained in me that I couldn't maintain a relationship with anyone.

Back in the States, Charlie and untold numbers of veterans found they had the same problem. They could not overcome this tendency to keep their distance from others. They knew they were doing it. The people around them were aware of it, but no one had any answers. Frustration set in and problems followed. Arguments broke out and feelings were hurt. Spouses or relatives desperate to gain or regain closeness with the veteran, thought that pointing out the problem would help. Instead, the veteran felt he had his nose rubbed in something he could not change.

The longer I live and the more I pursue relationships with people, the more I see that this is not just a "veteran thing." The tendency to stay hidden, even in close relationships, is much more common than I first believed. People from all over the world, in all walks of life, deal with similar issues in their relationships. It is especially true where one spouse has survived a traumatic event that has changed his life forever. Rape, assault, terrorism, hostage situations, rescue events—all of these—can forever change the life of one partner. Having survived unimaginable trauma, some cannot bridge the gap of experience that now isolates them from the people they once loved.

Occasionally I ask friends to give me feedback after reading my work. One of my friends wrote this response:

> I found it to be very interesting even though I am not a veteran. We (non-veterans) do the very same thing in our own lives with a little different twist. However, it is not only that we don't want the names of others, but also we don't want others to know our name. The theory is that if you don't know me, you can't hurt me. If you do hurt me, but I have never allowed you to know the real me, then I can brush it off as "it wasn't really me that hurt (or was rejected) because they never knew the real me."

My friend explained it this way: "It's all about protection, like you talked about in your description. I am protecting myself from pain by not getting to know you. The other side is that I am protecting myself from pain by not letting you know me."

Though the motive may be different, the effect remains the same. Both the veteran and the civilian miss out on the rich rewards of relationship.

It's my opinion that real relationships develop as we let it all hang out. When we let go of our self-protection, we become vulnerable (ouch...that can hurt). But without intimacy and its component vulnerability, we can never touch the genuine identity of another.

Deep inside, veterans, who have seen the worst in humankind, care deeply for other humans. But our fear—that we may once again lose someone we've grown close to—keeps us from getting close. It's as though we're human containers filled to the brim with losses, and to suffer one more may cause all those hurts to spill over the edge. The thought of enduring yet one more loss makes us afraid that we may lose control of our overflowing emotions. To do so might remove what little sanity we have left.

By keeping our relational distance, we effectively establish a demilitarized zone—a no-man's land. The distance becomes a kind of shock absorber to keep hurt at bay for both the vet and his loved ones. Unfortunately, keeping your distance is a battle-field operating procedure that renders us incapable of forming and keeping normal relationships.

Closeness, confidence and trust are key ingredients in normal human connections. The presence of a "buffer zone" keeps us from developing genuine and rewarding relationships.

Building Bridges

1. When you came home from the war, can you think of times that you felt betrayed? Who hurt you? The military? Your family? The press? The protestors? Can you remember an example?

2. How did you feel at the time?

3. Have you caught yourself remembering the hurt, reviewing it? Do you find yourself suspicious of others who might have the power to hurt you?

4. Have you ever felt the fear of losing someone you cared about? Who was it? What happened that made you feel that way?

5. Do you remember pulling away from someone, and sensing their disappointment? How did you know they were disappointed? What might you have done that would have felt safe for you, and yet made a way for closeness?

6. Is this definition of intimacy new to you? How is it different from your previous ideas? Does it make you uncomfortable to think that someone might know your dark side?

7. Can you think of one person you feel you can really trust? Could you safely share a bit more of yourself with them—even a small part? Could you tell them that you want to work on these issues? Could you ask for their help?

8. Could you ask for feedback? Would you be willing to have someone let you know when they sense you pulling away? Sometimes just being aware of our actions gives us the opportunity to make a healthier choice.

Chapter Seven

Night Vision
and Intimacy

There are three things that will endure—faith, hope, and love—and the greatest of these is love. Let love be your highest goal...

> Paul's first letter to the Corinthians
> (13:13–14:1 NLT)

Do you remember the last time you enjoyed a summer evening gazing at the stars? Did you notice anything odd about the starlight as you relished the beauty above you? Looking up, you may have discovered one of the more complex details of human physiology.

Beautiful as the stars may be against the black night, they are difficult to see clearly when you look directly at them. Why is that? Why do they seem to disappear when you look right at them, only to tease you again as you glance away?

This puzzling experience has to do with the placement of vision cells on the human retina. The cells responsible for night vision are located in a slightly off-center position, in the area of your peripheral vision. Because of this, you see things more clearly at night when you don't look directly at them.

Intimacy is a little like stargazing. It's easier to accomplish when you don't focus on it too directly. Consider this scene:

"Okay, you want intimacy," her husband begins, "let's be intimate." He moves his chair toward her, his knees touching hers.

"All right. You go first," she says, noticing the way his shoulders hug his ears and his hands clench the seat of the chair as though he were holding his body down against a tornado. This will never work, she thinks. *He'd rather have brain surgery without anesthesia.*

She's right. Most men feel that way about creating intimacy. To them, it seems like an impossible task. Even when they know that intimacy is vital to healthy relationships, most men don't have a clue about how to get there.

On the other hand, intimacy comes naturally to many women. Women tend to treasure and cultivate friendships. They feel comfortable being open with their lives. Women tend to value close relationships.

Men often mistake sexuality for intimacy. There is a great deal of truth in the old saying, "He trades intimacy for sex. She trades sex for intimacy."

In truth, sexual relationships can and do take place outside of an atmosphere of genuine intimacy. This is the nature of prostitution—the function of sexuality outside of relationship. It provides no lasting gratification and, even as it occurs, often feels demeaning and degrading to both partners.

The reverse is also true. Genuine intimacy *can* exist outside of sexual relationships. In fact, many friendships attain a level of trust and vulnerability that rivals the best marriages. Both men with men and women with women can achieve deep and intimate same-sex friendships. Where do they come from? Do people just decide to "make it happen?"

Rarely. In most cases, intimacy is the by-product rather than the objective of a relationship—just like seeing the stars is a by-product of looking at the night sky. Remarkably, focusing on another objective may be the most successful way to achieve intimacy.

The easiest way to build intimacy is to spend large amounts of time together. How individuals choose to make time for one another is not nearly as important as the amount of time together. In this case, more *is* better.

In time together, opportunity for conversation abounds. Conversation builds understanding between two people providing glimpses into one another's history. When we know what someone has survived, we feel more compassion for his choices, for his present situation. In casual conversations, two people share their own unique perspective on the world around them. In doing this, both persons have the opportunity to see the world in new ways.

Over time, with lots of conversation, two people begin to trust one another. They both believe that this friend will listen without judgment or correction or advice. They feel accepted— just as they are—and believe that they can reveal more and more of themselves in the safety of the relationship.

In fact, time spent together is such a valuable contribution to intimacy that I believe it to be the first step in many affairs. It happens all around us. Husbands commute to work with women other than their wives. Women work with men on long-range office projects. Whenever people spend lots of time together, the possibility of developing intimate ties exists. Often it happens before we are even aware of it.

Like a ballet, this ebb and flow of give and take, of share and trust, of reveal and accept builds into an intimate relationship. Most people believe it takes effort. I believe it happens naturally, over time. Lots and lots of time.

How do people create time for relationships to develop?

PHYSICAL GOALS

Whether the intimacy is between friends, or between couples, it follows much the same course. Some couples choose to work toward a physical goal together. The goal itself doesn't have to be dramatic or especially difficult. They may decide to walk the dog together every evening. Men may decide to run together every day, working toward a weight loss goal. I know a couple of women who ride bicycles long distances together, building toward a century ride.

Every evening I watch one couple work out together at our local fitness center. I know another couple who decided to learn to teach children to ski. They spent long winter weekends taking teaching classes. Though separated during class time, the weekly drive to the mountain gave them lots of time alone.

Spending time together builds intimacy.

PROJECTS TOGETHER

Years ago my husband and I worked hard to get an old house ready for sale. We spent hours painting and cleaning that little house. I trimmed along the floor with a small brush as he rolled gallons of paint on the wall behind me. We talked, we laughed, and we shared our experiences. Over time, covered in latex paint splatter, we grew together. Though we worked on a mundane task, we had time to talk, time to grow.

Maybe you need an addition on your house. Perhaps you could redecorate the family room. Maybe you could work with a friend on a project for your community or your church. Nearly anything will do. You only need to find a project that will take lots of time and provide ample opportunity for conversation.

COMMON GOALS

Working toward a common goal provides another opportunity to build intimacy. Consider community goals. Perhaps you'd like to help with the animal shelter "pet adoption day."

Maybe you'd like to restore a nature habitat in your county, or you might help raise funds for the rails to trails movement in your area. Maybe you'd like to help at a homeless shelter, or a food drive, or a Christmas toy drive. Perhaps you'd both like to help with literacy projects in your area, or you could both be part of a big sisters or big brothers program.

Perhaps you'd like to take on the youth group at your church or help with the winter production at your local community theatre. Maybe you both could volunteer to help disabled veterans.

Take time to choose a goal that evokes some passion in both of you. Make it something you care about, something you want to spend time working on. Choose something important to the future of your community.

Whenever the two of you take on a goal, you both become members of a team. The objective is suddenly something out there, something outside of yourselves. The difficulties you experience won't come from inside your relationship. As you work together, you will find yourself uniting to solve problems and overcome adversity in a new way. The lessons you learn, the skills you gain as you work together on an outside project will bolster your husband-wife relationship.

More than helping your community, or benefiting your church, you will learn to overcome conflicts in your relationship in a more objective and impersonal way. You won't be tempted to attach value judgments to the suggestions each of you offers as you solve problems together.

Most importantly, working together will make you more aware of the ways you value one another. The strengths you valued when you first met will become apparent again. Your trust in one another will rise to new heights. You will see your partner with new eyes and have new admiration for his abilities and skills.

TALKING TOGETHER

Not all talking moves a relationship forward, but there are some attitudes and skills that you can bring to your conversations that will help you build intimacy as you spend time together. When you and your partner talk, you can determine to build an atmosphere that fosters trust, vulnerability, and growth.

Acceptance

Every human is entitled to his own feelings and opinions and values. Your friend's unique viewpoint is part of what makes him different from every other human on the planet. When we accept others, we acknowledge their unique perspective and contribution to humanity. Though we may not always agree with them, we value what another human brings to the conversation, no matter how different our own perspective may be.

Acceptance is like respect. It means that nothing you tell me will shake my firm commitment to your value as a human. I know you aren't perfect. No one is. Still, I take you as you are and cherish your personhood.

When you accept someone, you accept that person's feelings about an event. You accept his fears and weaknesses. When someone you love tells you about their very bad day, you don't try to change their mind or convince them of another perspective. You don't begin a contest of "Can you top this?" You simply acknowledge their disappointment that things didn't turn out as well as they'd hoped. Your acceptance becomes a gift that helps to move the conversation forward.

Ask Questions

When we ask thoughtful questions, we show our genuine interest in what others have to say. Questions help to build intimacy by helping our partner feel listened to and valued. The right question can help others to uncover hidden feelings, or fears, or expectations. Often a carefully considered question can lead your friend to discover something hidden beneath their current concern—something they may not even be aware of. Try questions like these:

+ What did that feel like?
+ Where do you think that feeling came from?
+ What would you have liked to hear him say?
+ What might you have done differently?
+ How can I help you with that?

The well-placed question is a great intimacy builder. Of course, you can't ask good questions without first listening carefully to your friend. Listen for the feelings behind the words. What seems to be the *real* concern? If your partner is a survivor, watch carefully for the kinds of body language that will give you clues about your partner's feelings.

Nothing builds relationship like knowing the one you care for genuinely wants to hear what you have to say.

Telling the Truth

When two people talk, only complete honesty can help them grow closer together. This means that both partners are willing to admit what they are thinking or feeling. Admitting the truth requires that both partners are willing to be vulnerable.

Vulnerability is telling the truth about what is inside you—both the good and bad parts of your life and your experiences. You can only tell what you know. And you only know about yourself. In order to be vulnerable, you need to commit to being honest. You certainly cannot read your partner's mind. Neither can you know what is true about the inside of your partner.

Only you can be honest about your own life. Bob is a classic example:

Bob survived the battle for Hill 875 in November of 1967. Many experts considered this fighting the fiercest of the entire

Vietnam War. His body survived with only shrapnel wounds. But Bob found the damage to his psyche, the terror and daily tormenting guilt, a much larger burden to bear.

Before Vietnam, Bob maintained an active social life with numerous hobbies and interests. He was satisfied with the career choice he planned after his commitment as an officer in the U.S. Army. Bob seemed to know who he was, and felt connected to a variety of people. He loved and was fun-loving and creative in relationships.

Before he went overseas he had a satisfying life.

But after Hill 875 and his long months as an infantry officer in 'Nam ended, things changed. His view of himself changed— and he saw himself as much more vulnerable, not the strong person he used to be. He became anxious, stayed at home more, and became hesitant about taking risks. He also believed that others saw him differently because their friendship with him changed. He hadn't told most people about his experiences in combat. In fact, after the war, Bob did his best to portray the rugged individual he thought others expected of him.

He stuffed his past deep inside, figuring those memories were best left buried in his heart and mind. He believed they would go away on their own.

They didn't.

Bob lived in considerable fear and frustration, which he tried to control by keeping it to himself. The combination of fear and control interfered with his connection to others, and he began to feel increasingly alienated.

His self-esteem plummeted, and he became plagued with doubts about his manhood and identity. The activities that were meaningful to him before the war were replaced with a new pre-occupation. Bob simply wanted to get through the day. His sense of self was deeply shaken.

Some people who are alienated never break through to change. Fortunately Bob finally showed up at a support group meeting, and as the weeks went by, he found safety in a group of peers (other vets).

He began talking about his experiences, fears, weakness, and need for control. Just coming to the group wasn't enough. Bob found his way home by opening up to the deeper issues in his soul. When he became vulnerable, he found acceptance and healing.

BOUNDARIES

As you read this chapter, you may think that both partners must share every part of themselves with one another all the time. That kind of revelation would be tedious, confining.

A relationship is made of two separate and distinct persons. You must always give one another permission to draw whatever boundaries are necessary for the benefit of the individuals in the relationship and for the relationship itself. Sometimes, one of the partners may need some time away. At other times, a specific subject may be too painful to talk about. Occasionally, one of the partners may need time to think through an issue before responding to the questions or concerns of the other. Healthy adults give one another permission to say no, to set limits. These kinds of limits may actually help a relationship grow:

"No, I can't talk about that now."

"I need some time alone tonight."

"It hurts too much to talk about that. I need time to be quiet for a while."

Today people use the term "boundaries" to refer to the process of defining your own limits and respecting the limits of others. Boundaries may seem like the hot new subject for self-help books. But being able to have and keep boundaries is *especially* important for those who have been traumatized by their past.

Having already experienced demoralizing abuse and flagrant boundary busting by others, many survivors have difficulty avoiding future abuse. They have difficulty finding and keeping healthy boundaries. If you are feeling this way, you might want to read several of the excellent books on the topic, including *Boundaries* by John Townsend, and Henry Cloud.

The most important thing two people in relationship can do is to respect one another's boundaries. When your partner decides not to share any more, try not to view it as relational failure. Choose instead to use that opportunity to affirm your partner's individuality and growth.

By letting your partner set limits, and then by respecting his limits, you help your partner strengthen his sense of self. Your partner will feel more secure within the safety of these limits. You help your partner learn to trust you. At the same time, you demonstrate your commitment to his separateness and your desire to receive from him only what he feels comfortable giving.

TRUST

When two people begin to share their souls, misunderstandings always occur. Feelings can be hurt. To prevent that, I recommend that every couple commit to this one word: trust.

By this I mean, both partners assume the best of the other. They assume that their partner would not deliberately hurt them, wants the best for them, and wants the relationship to grow, to deepen, to improve.

These assumptions will prevent both partners from overreacting to the inevitable misunderstandings that come with our humanity. In assuming the best of your partner, you can ask questions without accusation. Simple questions such as, "I'm confused. What did you mean by that?" can be nonthreatening ways of clearing the air and getting the conversation back on target. With trust, misunderstandings cannot derail the process of building intimacy.

Acceptance

Questions

Vulnerability

Boundaries

Trust

These qualities will help even ordinary, everyday conversations grow your relationship into the rewarding friendship that you long to experience. Make the commitment together. You can do it.

BUILDING BRIDGES

1. Does the idea of building intimacy seem frightening to you? Exciting? Why?
2. Which of the intimacy builders seems most likely to work in your case?
3. What projects have you always longed to be involved in? Have you told your partner of your wishes?
4. Have you ever asked your partner how he or she might enjoy spending more time with you?
5. What might be the worst thing that could happen if you tried some of the ideas in this chapter?
6. If your spouse chose not to participate, how would you feel?
7. Do you know a safe person with whom you might build a better friendship?
8. Would you consider asking that person to join you for some activities together?

CHAPTER EIGHT

Finding Middle Ground

When conflict arises in interpersonal relationships—those
who insist on winning, eventually lose—and lose big.

I think that the only way we can prevent today's war—the war of struggling relationships—is to go back and resolve the wars of our past. Let me explain what I mean:

On the same morning that terrorists destroyed the World Trade Center, I sat in my biweekly focus group at the Veteran's Administration. Like the rest of our nation, our support group struggled with confusion and shock. With terrifying TV images swirling in our minds—of commercial jets piercing the twin towers, of a smoldering Pentagon and of people leaping from burning buildings—all we could do was sit and stare at one another. Anger and grief engulfed us.

Churning with unexpressed emotions, I had to let them out; I vented first. At the end of a torrent of anger, confusion, and the need for revenge, I slumped in the chair exasperated. I summarized with these words, "Things like this happen and all I want to do is kill someone! I don't want to feel like this; but I don't have the tools to think any other way. The Army never taught me how to find middle ground in conflicts. I don't know how to have a problem with someone and then stop and work it out so it has a good ending for everyone. It seems to me like someone always has to live and someone always has to die—there's no in-between."

Even as I said them, those words resonated with a kind of raw truth that startled me. I saw the same feelings reflected in the faces of the men around me. I had just put words to an issue we all struggled with. My comment made each of us realize how little we knew about making peace with people when they upset us.

In fact, those words made me decide to write this book.

In my six years as a soldier, two of them as a drill sergeant, I never once took a class about negotiating a peaceful resolution with anyone. No one instructed me in the area of compromise or problem solving. In war, we had only one objective: close on the enemy and eliminate him. When we could not overcome the enemy, we had only one response: retreat.

Destroy or pull back. From the beginning of wars, this is the military way. It was our training. It was all we knew. Take ground or give it up. Win or lose.

Live or die.

All of these military terms became the mantra by which we survived the worst years of our lives. Without these principles, we faced certain defeat. Only our mantra could bring us home alive.

But, when we returned to civilian life, we didn't let go of our old military thinking. When things got intense, we continued to resort to methods we knew best—fight like hell or run the other direction.

You don't have to be a therapist to see that this pattern doesn't promote lasting relationships in a civilian world. In fact this reaction, this defeat or retreat response, might be the reason so many Vietnam veterans are incarcerated today, charged with abuse and assault. Their only method of conflict resolution was to fight. As they fought, some of them let go of their rage, lost control and physically hurt someone.

While this solution is easy to recognize, other, more subtle solutions may actually be different facets of the same problem. Some veterans, though not in jail, continue living by the same defeat or retreat mantra. As they experience conflicts in their primary relationships, these men choose to run away. Abandoning the ones they loved, they end up hurting people emotionally, leaving their most important relationships in shambles.

Some of those who ran did so literally. They continue to live like hermits in desolate isolation. Others, especially those who tend to blame their partners, simply ran from relationship to relationship, leaving behind devastated people and ransacked emotions. Still others, those who stay in a relationship for a long time run away by giving up any sense of self. Though they remain in the relationship physically, they disconnect emotionally.

If you hear no other sentence in this whole book, hear this: *If, when you encounter conflict in relationships, your only solution is to win—then you will certainly lose.*

On the other hand, when retreat is your only tool for handling conflict, you also lose.

In healthy relationships, we don't seek to *avoid* conflicts but rather to *resolve* them. In the process, if things go well, relationships are strengthened—not crippled; both partners come away with a stronger understanding of themselves and of the one we love. Working together, we find a solution that makes both of us happier than the solution we proposed to begin with.

If the process is healthy, our commitment to one another is strengthened as well. When we solve problems well, our partner's love for us isn't just something we hear about, it becomes something we *experience*. We know our partner cares, because we see that concern in action.

When we resolve conflicts successfully, we come away feeling like a team who has tackled and overcome an adversary *together*. Our relationship is stronger as a result, and we have an enhanced feeling of closeness.

As combat veterans, though our patterns of defeat and retreat may be firmly entrenched, they can be changed. All trauma sufferers (even those who are not veterans) who have had to fight the war of coping and adjusting to "normal life" after their traumatic experiences can change their relationship habits. We can choose to learn new conflict resolution skills. We can make the days ahead more productive and pleasant for everyone involved. But the choice is ours.

We can either ignore our deteriorating relationships with the people we care about, or we can forge new paths to middle ground. As we do, we will move a long way toward developing and sustaining good, healthy relationships—relationships not threatened by conflict.

You should know that finding middle ground is a difficult skill for all adults involved in close relationships. After a single Info Track search at my library, I turned up hundreds of articles on conflict management. Most everyone has something to learn about solving conflict.

The skills we suggest here are not original. We didn't make them up; instead, we've chosen to distill the most important ideas into bite-sized pieces. We've chosen to address those skills most affected by life-altering traumatic experiences. We'll show you how conflict resolution looks in healthy relationships. Then, we'll talk about how our training, habits, and unhealthy coping mechanisms may derail the process.

Solving conflicts is a matter of life and death. Social life, or social death…I hope you choose life.

So, how do we do it? How do we find middle ground? The five most important steps to finding middle ground are these: listen, speak, explore, choose, and evaluate.

LISTEN

Battles begin when two people want different things. She may want you to hang up your wet bath towels; you want her to stop complaining and pick them up herself. You may want to take a second job; she wants you to spend more time with her. Your different desires propel you toward conflict. Learning to listen is the first and most important thing you can do to diffuse the escalating tension in relationships.

Why listen? Even when you think you know what your spouse wants, by listening carefully you will find more beneath her request than meets the eye. Usually your partner's request is connected to an emotion, perhaps insecurity, a frustration, or a fear. Listening will help you discover the underlying concern. It will help you look for solutions that address the real problem—rather than the superficial issue that escalates into an argument.

Listening involves time—time for a heart-to-heart discussion. You must both approach this conversation with love and respect. Conflict resolution skills work only if you will maintain an open and nondefensive manner. In her article, "Intimacy: the Art of Working Out Your Relationships," (*Psychology Today*, September 1993, Volume 26, No. 5,) Lori Gordon stresses the importance of listening:

> The single biggest barrier to such empathetic listening is our self-interest and self-protective mechanisms. We anticipate and fill in the blanks. One of the simple truths of relationships is that often enough, all we need to do to resolve a problem is to listen to our partner—not just passively listen but truly hear what is in the mind and in the heart…Instead of focusing on the effects of your partner's words on you, pay attention instead to your partner's emotions, facial expressions and levels of tension.

For instance, as you listen to the underlying emotions, you may discover surprising motivations like these: While she asks for more time together, underneath she may be saying something much more important, like, "I'm afraid that you don't love me like you used to." Or, "I don't feel valued as a woman anymore. To you, I'm only the mother of your kids." Or, "I'm afraid about all the time you spend with the women at your work. I'd like to have more time together, so that I can feel more confident of your love for me."

You can't find middle ground until you really hear what he or she wants and begin to understand why their desire is so important to them. This takes time and patience. As you listen make these commitments:

Don't interrupt. Let her say everything she wants to—no matter how long it takes or how painful her words are for you to hear.

Try to summarize. After he finishes, try to restate his concerns in just a few sentences. If you cannot summarize, ask questions about the parts you don't understand and then listen again with the same intensity and compassion you did before. Continue listening and summarizing until he feels confident that you have genuinely heard his concerns.

SPEAK

Now it's your turn to explain how you feel about the conflict.

Why do you want what you want?

What are you feeling about it?

How would you feel if you didn't get your own way?

Why does the issue mean so much to you?

Is there an emotion boiling around under the surface for you? What is it? Fear? Jealousy? Anger? Confusion? Insecurity? Embarrassment?

As you speak, try to be as specific as you can—without accusing or belittling your partner. Remember, this is your opportunity to talk only about your own perspective. Avoid phrases like "you always," or "you never." If you are really presenting your own perspective, you will use the word "I," rather than the word, "you."

When you have finished, ask your partner if he has any questions. Ask him if he would like to paraphrase what you have said. From his summary, decide whether or not he heard what you meant to tell him. If not, gently and patiently try again.

EXPLORE

Exploration can be an exciting and rewarding part of conflict resolution. Rarely do problems come with only two solutions—his or hers. Instead, there are often many options which might give each partner what he or she wants.

At this stage, take out a piece of paper and write down as many of those solutions as you can. Do it quickly, without evaluating the ideas as you go along. Simply write them down. At this point, more is better. Even if they seem impossible or illogical, something you have written may trigger a more reasonable or workable approach later.

Right now, your only goal is to get lots of ideas on paper.

CHOOSE

You may want to take a break from brainstorming and think about your options for a couple of days before you move on to this next step. You may even need to diffuse some emotional tension. When the two of you finally decide which option you want to implement, be certain that your decision considers the real needs and wants of both partners. Realize that choosing may not be the end of the discussion. Choosing is simply a step.

Once you make a decision, you may try it for a week, or a month, with the plan of re-evaluating the solution at some later date. Implementing the solution on a trial basis may help it seem less threatening to both partners. Try phrasing the solution in these terms. "We'll walk the dog together after dinner for a week and see if we like that."

Be certain to set a time limit for the solution, and to plan time for the next step.

Evaluate

When the prescribed time frame has passed, evaluate the results. If one of you remains dissatisfied, you may want to go back to the listening step. Find out why the solution was not satisfactory. See if any new concerns have come up since your last discussion. Reflect on your own feelings. Make a different choice, or make a new list of choices and try again.

If this process feels threatening to you, you can start using these conflict resolution skills at work or with friends. Start with decisions as small where to play tennis or what movie to see. Later, after you practice with less threatening issues, you can use these skills on more important decisions with your spouse or closest friends.

When you do, fill your discussions with respect and caring. Don't be afraid to share a laugh together in the process. When one of you feels your emotions swinging out of control, be sure to take a "time out."

As you take the break, always schedule a time to resume the discussion. Try something like this: "I'm feeling a little scared right now. Let's take a break and pick this up after dinner."

After you have tried these suggestions, choose a time when you are not under any stress and spend some time evaluating the process itself. Ask questions of one another. Were you satisfied with the way things went? What might we have done that would make you feel better about the process? With practice and reflection, you will find that you *can* solve conflict in a way that satisfies both of you.

Building Bridges

1. Can you think of a conversation when someone made you feel really listened to? Can you picture the conversation? What did the person do that had that effect? How did they sit? Did they speak? When? How? What did they say that helped you know that you had been heard?

2. Can you remember a time when someone you loved wanted to solve a problem and your anger got in the way of a solution? If you could go back now, what might you do differently to change the outcome?

3. What time of day are you most likely to stay in control, producing a loving, respectful discussion as you work toward resolution? Is there a time of day when one of you turns into a gorilla? Can you agree not to disagree at that time of day?

4. Can you think of ways your partner can help you build these new skills? Would it help to schedule your conversations ahead of time? Would a different time of day be more effective—or less volatile? Would it help to go out for coffee or to the park? Is there something your partner says regularly that makes it especially hard for you to act respectfully?

5. Can you think of one small (easy) conflict where you would like to try these skills? Begin with a paper and pencil. Jot down a few details about your desires. What is the conflict about? What is it that you want? Why is that important to you? When your own exploration is finished, can you commit to really listen to your partner's concerns?

CHAPTER NINE

What's So
Hard about
Middle Ground?

*Boys with a normal viewpoint were taken from the fields
and offices and factories and classrooms and put into the
ranks. There they were remolded; they were made over;
they were made to "about face," to regard murder as the
order of the day. They were put shoulder to shoulder, and
through mass psychology they were entirely changed. We
used them for a couple of years and trained them to think
nothing at all of killing or of being killed. Then suddenly,
we discharged them and told them to make another "about
face." This time they had to do their own readjusting (without) mass psychology, (without) officers' aid and advice,
(without) nation-wide propaganda. We didn't need them
any more. So we scattered them about without any speeches
or parades. Many, too many, of these fine young boys are
eventually destroyed mentally, because they could not make
that final "about face" alone.*

1936, Smedley D. Butler, Major General, USMC
Two-time winner, Congressional Medal of Honor

While it helps to understand the basics of successful conflict resolution, no discussion of these skills would be complete without trying to fully understand why conflict resolution is so extremely difficult for survivors of trauma.

Granted, everyone struggles with resolving conflict. It begins in our childhood. Ever observe a two-year-old in the grocery store? Pointing to the goodies lining the shelves, the toddler asks over and over, "Mommy, please?"

What about the preschooler who loses his favorite toy to a playmate? "Mine!" he screams, pulling with all his might to retrieve the beloved item. Even now, thinking about some of the childhood battles I've observed, I cringe.

Children may grow up, but even as adults, we want what we want. But why do combat veterans have a harder time with conflict than other adults? Let's explore the issue as it relates specifically to men who have survived the trauma of war.

Don't Ask Questions!

The military tradition of rank and obedience may contribute to the problem. In the military, soldiers don't make decisions as equals. Soldiers don't hear the reasoning behind the orders they receive. They don't discuss their feelings about a decision. They don't consider the alternatives to an order and pick the one they feel comfortable with. Soldiers get an order and follow it. Soldiers simply obey.

Soldiers expect the same obedience of the men ranked below them. When a man gives an order, he doesn't expect to have to explain himself, or to listen to anyone's feelings about the order. Soldiers expect obedience. Military men often carry this concept into their personal lives. We've all heard of the commander who tries to parent his children as though they were in boot camp.

That kind of parenting doesn't work with children. And it is especially detrimental to interpersonal relationships. If you care about your spouse, you must value her needs and wants. Her viewpoints and insights must be considered as important as your own—because they are. A good relationship between two humans has nothing to do with rank. Whether friendship or marriage, lasting relationships are formed by equals.

Rambo Solves a Problem

Another way our combat training may interfere with conflict resolution has to do with human biology. Though it sounds boring, hang in there with me for a minute. As we strive for a peaceful resolution of conflict, we need to understand something about adrenaline—the "juice" that drives most of us from day to day. It also gets us into trouble in our relationships.

Without getting too wordy or technical I'll try to explain how it works:

God designed us for survival, equipping us with adrenal glands located on the top of each kidney. These tiny glands are stimulated by our nervous system when we get upset or frightened. In response, they secrete survival hormones. These chemicals pour into the bloodstream giving us new energy and strength to overcome the perceived danger. This sudden flow of hormones makes us stronger, and more alert. They protect us from blood loss, increase our lung capacity, focus our vision, and direct blood flow away from unnecessary organ functions to the large muscles of the body.

Physiologists call this collection of physical changes the "fight or flight" response. They enable a frightened husband to lift the car off his injured wife; or they allow a terrified woman to run long distances for help. With this system fully functioning, our physical capacity for exceptional performance borders on the supernatural.

While this system keeps us alive in the face of extraordinary danger, it does have one major flaw. The reactive portion of the human brain cannot differentiate between a real threat and an imagined one! The brain doesn't notice or care if it has encountered something real or a memory stimulated from something around us. Determined to keep us safe, it simply sends out the urgent signal to react. The adrenaline flows, and we function with an "out of body" response.

Adrenaline flowing from a "false need" can be dangerous to our own health as well as to our relationships with loved ones, friends, and people in general. Not only does adrenaline put extra stress on critical body organs—like the heart and circulatory system—but the constant presence of adrenaline can be addictive—nearly as addictive as an illegal drug.

In relationships, the adrenaline response almost always works against us. Once the process begins, adrenaline is nearly impossible to control—especially after months of combat, where our survival depended on adrenaline for prolonged periods of time. Our body becomes used to and extremely efficient in starting and responding to the adrenaline response. What was meant to be a response for crisis becomes a way of life.

In human relationships, the adrenaline cycle can send us down two equally destructive pathways.

You've heard about the combat veteran who suddenly dives for cover when he hears a car backfire or fireworks explode. The noise signals danger; his brain, unable to differentiate between a real or imagined threat, begins the adrenaline cycle. An old imprinted message tells him to move into action and survive. Without thinking, he responds just as he did in combat. Most of the time, his response is inappropriate for peacetime situations.

The trigger can be a smell, a sound, or any combination of some fifty other sensory perceptions that may be associated with a past threat or injury. When these sudden triggers occur, the veteran may suffer tremendous emotional upset. The fear, pain, helplessness, and confusion of his wartime experiences surface immediately.

When this cycle happens in the presence of those close to the veteran, they too are affected by his behavior. They may feel frustrated because they don't understand or can't help. This kind of episode embarrasses the unsuspecting veteran, just as it does the victim of severe trauma. His confused partner may even blame herself for the event.

To protect himself and those close to him, the survivor may separate himself even further. As the survivor considers the trigger, he may generalize his experience, refusing to talk about the issue while determined to avoid any similar stimulation. His (the survivor's) emotional withdrawal and physical isolation now combine with his partner's confusion about the event. In the end, this destructive pattern further diminishes the chance of sustaining a healthy relationship.

In the other pathway, the flowing adrenaline produces a kind of hormonally induced "high." When trauma survivors, and especially combat veterans, experience this adrenaline flow over and over in the presence of conflict—a response that was perfectly acceptable in a time of danger or the heat of battle—the resulting "high" they experience becomes rewarding in itself.

This high, the rage generated by conflict, can become a pattern, burned into the brain like a computer burns a CD. It can become as rewarding as the high of drugs or alcohol. Rage can lead to irrational behavior or acts of violence expressed against anyone—even those he loves.

This hormonally induced rage can stimulate the kind of violence that puts many veterans in jail.

Rage has no place in conflict resolution.

Anger that erupts into rage stimulates a kind of "fight or flight" cycle. This escalates the hormonal response of the body.

The hormones in turn stimulate more rage. As the body prepares for a Rambo-type chase scene, our ability to listen, to reason, to communicate, takes a flight of its own. With building rage, our humanity becomes inaccessible.

In finding middle ground, we must learn to short-circuit our rage. Unless we do, we will frighten away everyone we love or care about, leaving ourselves alone and isolated. In severe addictions, rage can lead to devastating consequences including murder.

There are many ways to short-circuit the process. Let me suggest a few. Begin paying attention to your body as you experience the first feelings of anger. Do your jaw muscles tighten? Do your hands grow cold? Does your breath come in little puffs? Associate those physical sensations with your increasing tension, and use them as a signal to take a break.

Don't be afraid to say, "I need to take a break right now. Let's discuss this later." This is perfectly acceptable, whether you are talking with the boss, your wife, or the customer relations manager for the phone company.

Don't let your anger build to the point that it feeds the adrenaline cycle. If you are with a stranger, take yourself away physically. Leave the room. Get off the freeway. Hang up the phone. Do whatever you need to do to remove yourself from the stimulus *before* the cycle begins. After you withdraw, work to relax. Take deep breaths. Take your your mind off the conflict, and on to something positive. Consider exercise as a means to burn off accumulating adrenaline. Take a walk or go for a run. Only when you are back in control should you try again to solve that issue. The longer you go between cycles of rage, the less power rage holds over you.

READ MY MIND

Like most veterans, I dislike crowded places. Once, in spite of my discomfort, I took my three sons to the mall.

As the crowd swelled around us, I lost sight of the boys and began to get nervous. When I finally caught sight of them, I found myself giving them hand signals as if we were on patrol. They didn't have a clue what I was trying to do. Moments later, they headed off in three different directions and disappeared. Why did they ignore my signals?

I found a bench in the center of the mall and waited, fighting for control. Eventually they showed up, completely oblivious to my distress. I had to hold my tongue. Inside I wanted to put my U.S. Army drill instructor hat on and line them up and scream in their faces, "What's wrong with you? Don't you know the signals?" But I managed to hold it together. To this day, I don't think any of them know how difficult that day was for me.

The anxiety came from my combat training. Working together day in and day out, soldiers learn to survive in hostile territory by getting "in tune" with one another. Eye movements, body signals, and sudden changes in the body language of your companions meant life or death to you. Reading each other ensured the effectiveness of the mission and the safety of the entire team.

That's good news and bad news.

The bad news? Your family, especially your spouse or loved one, probably has no clue what you are trying to tell them with your body signals. You cannot depend on these silent signals to transmit your message. You must learn to tell the ones you love what they need to hear. You must believe that your loved ones want to hear your concerns.

The good news? Having learned to watch others so carefully, you already have an important skill firmly established. When you listen to your spouse, you can watch for signals that confirm or deny the words she speaks. You, more than many men in our culture, can tune in to a quivering lip, crossed arms, or an averted gaze. You can use your observations to gather reconnaissance data about the critical issues your family faces.

Then, you can ask appropriate questions to confirm your observations. Questions like these: "You look sad. Have I hurt you in some way?" Or, "You seem frustrated. What can I do to help with that?" or "You seem really tense. How can I help ease your tension?"

In my healing process, I have found over and over again that the more I learn about something, the easier it is to change. The same is true in relationships. We must go back to square one and find out what isn't working and why. Not only must we learn new skills for conflict resolution, we must also understand why we have developed so many nonfunctional skills.

As we observe ourselves in the process of solving conflict, we can see the destructive pathways created by our combat training. Then we can choose to change direction. We can learn the mechanics of finding middle ground and begin to apply them in our most valued relationships.

As we apply both our new understanding and advanced skills, we can begin to uncover the missing peace in our lives.

BUILDING BRIDGES

1. Have you ever found yourself expecting unquestioning obedience from others in civilian life?
2. Can you remember how they responded when you issued "orders?"
3. Did your relationship change as you exerted your rank over others? What happened?
4. Have you ever issued orders to family members? Can you remember how they responded? How did their response make you feel?
5. Have you ever found yourself stuck trying to solve a conflict with someone you loved? Looking back, did one of the issues in this chapter make that conflict more difficult

to resolve? Which was it? What might you have done differently?

6. Can you think of a time when you expected someone else to read your mind? Were they able to? How did that feel?

7. What one quality of your conflict resolution style would you like to change?

8. What one behavior could you implement to begin the transformation?

9. Who could you tell about your desire to change?

CHAPTER TEN

Self-Talk

Most of the time, we aren't even aware of the chatter in our head. At other times…it becomes so loud that we wonder if those near us can hear it too.

Recreational salmon fishing is a favorite activity here in the Pacific Northwest. I don't get to go fishing often, but when I do, I love the salt air and the great views of nearby mountains.

When we're out on the water, we always keep our VHS radio on, listening for the fishermen hailing each other from nearby boats. Generally, the endless chatter on the radio is meaningless. But more than once, we've listened while the Coast Guard begins rescue operations for the waterlogged operators of overturned kayaks, or powerless boats drifting into commercial traffic lanes. What begins as chatter becomes a matter of life or death, rescue or drowning.

Every day, twenty-four hours a day, all of us listen to a radio of another sort. Like the VHS, this radio is cluttered with endless chatter, most of it inconsequential. Some of it though, is important enough to determine the course of our relationships.

This is the radio of our mind.

Psychologists refer to our mental chatter as "self-talk." You know it as the kind of verbal gibberish that swirls through your head all day long. You might have spoken to yourself with phrases like these:

"Oh shoot, I forgot the keys."

"Who would wear something like that to the grocery store?"

"Hasn't that guy ever heard of signaling?"

"I wonder if my check is in today's mail."

Most of the time, we aren't even aware of the chatter in our head. At other times, in the face of extreme emotions, like anger or grief, the chatter becomes so loud that we wonder if those near us can hear it too.

For most of us, how we talk to ourselves begins in childhood. Our early environment had a profound influence on what we believe to be true about ourselves. Culture, language, family life, touching, and sibling rivalry all play a part in our early sense of personhood.

These early experiences collectively shape our belief system. From them, we know who we are. We have strong feelings about whether or not we are physically attractive, mentally, musically, or athletically gifted. We believe that we can succeed or fail, that people can or cannot be trusted, that our love is secure, or that loved ones will eventually leave us. Such severe conclusions come to most children very early in life.

But in the case of trauma—like war, or assault, or crime, or even natural disaster—these belief systems can continue to shift long after most have normally settled. A previously trusting child, when attacked by a mugger at the age of twenty, can shift her belief system to include a profound sense of personal insecurity. Having survived a severe burn, a physically attractive woman might reshape her own sense of self to include deep shame.

What we believe about ourselves and our world, as well as our conclusions about life, are reflected in the verbal chatter flitting through our thoughts.

"I can never succeed in business."

"Women cannot be trusted."

"He'll eventually leave, just like all the others."

"The government doesn't really care about me."

"I can't deal with conflict."

When these conclusions collide with the events and circumstances in our lives, our emotions come alive. If we believe we are inept when it comes to business, and then are fired from a job, we see the firing as a reflection of our failure. The self-talk escalates. "I shouldn't have taken that job. I knew I'd blow it. I'm such a failure."

We begin to feel hopeless, depressed, and afraid to try again. The more our self-talk escalates, the more our emotions render us impotent, frozen, unable to make the very decisions that might lead us toward a genuine change.

Most of us believe that action affects outcome. If you want to do well in school, you must study. If you want to lose weight, you must exercise. If you want healthy relationships, you must work to make them better.

And while these statements are true, it is also true that our actions begin at a much deeper level. Actions originate in our thought life. Our thoughts are a reflection of what we believe to be true about the events and people surrounding us.

Let me go through a simple example:

You have overslept. You pull out of your driveway seventeen minutes late for a very important meeting with your boss. As you drive toward the freeway, these sentences float through your mind: *I can't believe the alarm didn't go off. My boss is going to think I don't care about this meeting. He's going to think that my job doesn't mean anything to me. Man, if I don't make up some time on the way to work, I might as well not go in. I'm going to get fired anyway.*

As you merge onto the freeway, you glance at your watch. A guy in a red Explorer slides in behind you and zooms by on the left. You narrowly avoid an accident. *Who does that guy think he is, driving like that? I can't believe the selfishness of all these guys on the freeway. Everyone out for themselves. No one gives a rip about anyone any more. Man, it's a dog-eat-dog world. That guy cut me off on purpose. He saw me there. He knew I was trying to get on the freeway.*

The more you think about the red Explorer, the angrier you feel. Your foot begins to push harder on the accelerator, and you begin driving as though you are a NASCAR winner. Determined not to let other drivers take advantage of you, you cut off a tractor-trailer rig as you zip around him headed for your freeway exit.

Your actions—in this case, irresponsible driving—are fueled by angry emotions. The emotions come directly from the thoughts and conclusions you have been telling yourself from the moment you climbed out of bed. Each dire prediction builds upon another until you have left yourself with no option but to jump off the cliff with your own imaginary conclusion.

How many of us have lived through a morning like this only to arrive at the office and find a note taped to our computer screen saying, "Meeting canceled. Jim overslept. Sorry."

These same thoughts and conclusions fuel the struggles we face with the ones we love. Parents talk themselves into sweating terrors when a child is late from school. Wives talk themselves into frantic tears when they find an unexplained phone number on the long distance telephone bill.

Beginning with the simplest of conflicts, our own parade of self-talk can escalate a misunderstanding into a world war. The simplest of these mistakes can seem hilariously funny. But the serious ones can leave relationships unalterably damaged before the misunderstanding is cleared. We must prevent the problem before minor disagreements escalate into nuclear holocaust.

We avoid these kinds of escalations by controlling our self-talk. Consider these four keys to controlling the words you say to yourself:

Become aware of the chatter: As a first step in controlling the words flying through your mind, begin to pay attention to your own inner dialogue. Listen carefully to the words you speak to yourself. Don't try to change anything just yet. Just listen. Pay extra attention to the words you hear whenever you feel your emotions rise. No matter what emotion you feel, anger, fear, frustration, irritation, let it make you very attentive to the words floating through your mind. Listen carefully. In those words, you will often discover the keys to your own actions and emotions.

Begin to ask yourself doubting questions. As you hear these phrases float through your mind, begin to questions them. In the example about the man who is late for his meeting, questions might include: Will I really get fired if I'm late for this meeting? Doesn't everyone over sleep occasionally? Did that driver really intend to cut me off? I wonder if he saw the traffic clearly?

The point here is to slow down the flow of your self-talk. By asking questions you have excused yourself from the position of prosecutor, judge, and jury. Rather than allowing each statement to escalate your emotions, fueling your anger or frustration, you can begin to turn the tide of your unreasonable response. You will begin to see things more clearly and at the same time, de-escalate the intensity of the emotions you feel.

Your doubting questions will point out how much you really don't know about a situation that you feel strongly about. As you recognize these inaccurate conclusions floating through your mind, you can begin to set aside the chain of thoughts that follow them.

In many cases, this simple commitment can deescalate the intense emotions you might be feeling in a tense situation.

In examining my own self-talk, I've discovered that much of it is based on assumptions. I've found that I often assume things about the motives of others. I assume that others know things about me and about my desires. As I escalate these assumptions, building one upon the other, I find my emotions spiraling wildly out of control.

I've learned that for me, doubting my self-talk means more than asking doubting questions. I've found that I must assume that my own assumptions are wrong!

Begin to ask for clarification. Self-talk occurs all the time—when we are late for work, when our wives accuse us of over-disciplining the children, when we forget where we left our car keys. In the case of interpersonal conflict, a virtual river of self-talk flows through our thoughts as we try to solve problems. The nature of the statements may change, but the flow has the same effect. We become prosecutor, judge, and jury, and our opponent no longer has the opportunity to solve the problem *with* us. Instead, we sentence those we love to the prison of rejection and misunderstanding.

As you argue with your wife, your self-talk might include snippets like these: *She said that to hurt me. She has always thought I was nuts. This proves it. She never appreciates anything I do for her.*

Asking for clarification takes your fight against destructive self-talk a step further. For instance, on the day that your wife makes navy bean soup for dinner, you may find yourself feeling irritable or even angry. You may hear thoughts like these: *she knows I hate this soup. But she made it anyway. She doesn't really care what I think.* Your thoughts continue to spiral downward until you find yourself acting out your irritation or even expressing outright anger. How do you stop it?

As soon as the thought trail begins, ask your partner some clarifying questions.

"Honey, I'm wondering if you remembered how much I really hate navy bean soup?"

You might discover that she did remember, but that she had to spend the last of the grocery budget on an unexpected prescription, or that she's been to the doctor and her cholesterol count demands a meatless diet.

As simple as this example seems, asking questions can defuse even the most anxious moments of interpersonal conflict.

Begin to take control of what you tell yourself. Until I began to think about the things I tell myself, it never occurred to me that I *could* control the flow of thoughts raging through my overactive brain. Now I realize that not only can I be aware of what I'm telling myself—I can *change* it.

As I make these changes, I find that my actions and attitudes change as well.

Let's go back to the example of being late for work. Think how differently that morning might have felt if I began saying these kinds of things to myself: *It was a mistake to oversleep, but everyone makes mistakes. My boss might be frustrated with me, but we can reschedule the meeting if we have to. I do good work and make an important contribution to my company. This one mistake won't undo all the things I've done well. I'll do my best to get to work as quickly as possible, but I won't endanger others. Man, that guy in the Ford must be having a bad morning. He didn't even notice my signal.*

These kinds of statements—statements that reflect the truth and which take control of the thoughts raging through your mind—have a powerful ability to direct both your attitudes and behavior toward other people. At the same time, by controlling your thoughts you begin to control your emotions as well.

In the case of conflict with your wife, your changed thoughts might sound like this: *Oh man, I hate navy bean soup, but I think my wife knows that. She loves me. Something pretty important must have led to this choice. I wonder what happened. I'll make time to talk about the menu later. When we talk, she can tell me what really happened in her world today. Oh well, I can stand soup for one evening.*

These are the kinds of things that can help you to *understand* your partner or friend rather than to *judge* them as uncaring or hurtful. Controlling the things you tell yourself will go a long way toward building safe and healthy relationships with those around you.

Begin telling yourself the things you would like to be true. Now you have taken control of your self-talk a step further. For many years, sports psychologists, weight control experts, and drug and alcohol rehabilitation programs have known and incorporated this truth in to their programs.

Whether bad or good, what you tell yourself becomes *the truth.*

So why not tell yourself what you want to be true—so that over time, it can become the reality you experience.

If you are impatient during conflict, begin to tell yourself something different. Try words like this: *I love my wife; because of this, I am patient while she talks. I listen carefully and together we solve problems with kindness and compassion.*

If you tend to mistrust people in authority, you might try this: *I believe that my boss wants the best for me and for our company. Because of this, I believe the things he tells me. I accept his words at face value. I don't look for hidden meanings or double messages. If he wants to tell me something, I believe he will do so directly. If I have questions about his word, I will ask him directly. I do not assume he is out to get me.*

Just today, during a tennis game, I heard myself say disparaging things about my serve. I heard the self-talk, and decided to speak to myself differently: *I can serve the ball. I have a nice, easy toss, and I can accurately place the ball in the service box.* Not surprisingly, the ball began to go where I told myself to put it.

My self-talk actually changed my performance. It can change your behavior as well. More importantly, in the process of changing your self-talk, you can change the way you feel about your interaction with others.

Try these techniques. Become aware of the things you say to yourself, then apply your willpower to change your self-talk. Watch as your emotions and actions fall into line with the goals you have for your relationships with others. This is an important key for those whose lives have been affected by trauma or war.

Building Bridges

1. Have you ever paid attention to the litany of words flowing through your brain?

2. When you feel discouraged about your performance, or your ability to change, what kinds of things do you tell yourself? Could you record those thoughts for a couple of days?

3. In the past, when relationships went badly, what things did you tell yourself about another person's motives? Do you remember the words? Looking back, do you think the things you told yourself were true?

4. Have you ever made an attempt to change the way you talk to yourself about any particular area? Weight control? Substance abuse? What happened when you did?

CHAPTER ELEVEN

The Power of Honesty

We must choose to remove our partner's mistakes from the arena of our relationship. To do so brings healing and growth.

I have a friend who worked the burn unit at Harborview Hospital in Seattle, Washington. Her patients, people of all ages, suffered extensive burns caused by a wide range of injuries. Some had been in car accidents. Others used gasoline to start their barbecues. Many were fire fighters injured in the line of duty.

But for all of them, the healing process had one thing in common. Before healthy tissue could be grafted onto their wound, the burned tissue had to be completely removed.

Depending on the size of the burn, the debridement process (the process of removing the dead tissue) could take weeks. In those days, it often began with lengthy soaks in sterile tanks, followed by lengthy and arduous procedures done by therapists to remove tissue. Sometimes, a stream of high-pressure water shot directly at the burn washed off chunks of debris. Other times, wet gauze dressings were left to dry on the burn. When nurses stripped the dressings from the injured area, the dead tissue came off with them. Frequently, the last bits of skin had to be removed one tiny piece at a time with sterile forceps and gauze pads.

Needless to say, the procedure was excruciatingly painful. My friend, a physical therapist, tells me that the wounded often greeted her with vile cursing as soon as she opened the door to their rooms. They knew what she'd come to do, and they dreaded it. Though they'd been medicated in anticipation of her arrival, they associated her presence with intense pain.

Still it had to be done. No skin graft can grow on anything less than a healthy, well-vascularized skin bed. In the end, removing the dead stuff paved the way for healthy new skin to grow.

The same is true in relationships.

In relationships, mistakes are like the dead tissue on burn patients. Leaving our mistakes behind blocks growth—just like dead tissue blocks healing. We must remove the mistakes in our relationships if we hope for any growth.

We all make mistakes. We talk when we ought to listen. We strike out when we feel frightened or threatened. We retaliate when we feel betrayed. We withdraw when the one we love needs us most. We try to control our loved ones in an effort to make ourselves more comfortable, more secure—less scary.

We make mistakes.

But how can we remove mistakes? We can't take back our words. We can't rewind the clock. Sometimes, even if we could redo the event, we wouldn't know how to make things right. How can we remove the damage caused by our own humanity?

The process begins with personal responsibility.

In our day and age, personal responsibility isn't a popular term. We live in a world where passing the buck has become a requirement for professional businessmen. We learn early to deny our wrongdoing. We specialize in phrases like: "I didn't know." "I couldn't help it." Sometimes, we even lie about our mistakes—denying our participation in the injury.

At other times, we hide our responsibility behind our background or our upbringing. We live in a world where we cloak responsibility with words that end with *-aholism*—*workaholism*, *alcoholism*, *foodaholism*. Sometimes, we use prior hurts as excuses for assault and murder.

In relationships, personal responsibility means admitting when you are wrong. The irony is that nothing diffuses conflict like owning your mistakes.

"You're right. I was late getting here to pick you up. I'm sorry."

"You're right. I pulled away. I knew that you needed me, and I just wasn't there for you."

"You're right. I felt like I was loosing the argument, so I let go of my temper. I said things I shouldn't have said. I'm sorry."

In healthy relationships, not only do partners freely admit their mistakes, but they do something more. When one partner owns his mistake, the other chooses to remove the offense from the realm of the relationship. Between these partners, it is as if the offense never happened. This is the way healthy relationships stay clean—rather than being buried by the constant onslaught of repeated hurts.

Forgiveness is choosing to put aside our partner's mistakes. Without it, no relationship can thrive.

To go back to our burn unit illustration: When we choose not to forgive, we are like the burn patient, whose nurse points out the dead tissue and then decides to let the stuff remain where it was. In the burn unit, a fairly small injury—left unattended—becomes host to bacteria. In the end, infection causes widespread death to neighboring tissue. This sometimes leads to amputation, or in the worst cases, even the death of the patient.

Unforgiven blunders, like dead tissue, eventually putrefy. As the hurts decay, the healthy parts of the relationship also begin to die. In relationships, this decay can lead to divorce. It can end friendships and tear apart families.

We must choose to remove our partner's mistakes from the arena of our relationship. To do so brings healing and growth. When we extend forgiveness for the errors of others, we effectively break ground for experiencing forgiveness for our own mistakes.

Why is this so difficult? What keeps us from admitting our mistakes?

For all of us, covering our mistakes is part of the dark side of our human nature. It is the human way. What parent hasn't asked the kids, "Who spilled chocolate milk in the family room?" Only to hear a chorus of little voices chiming. "Not me!" (Dramatic finger pointing and loud blaming usually follows this exclamation.)

Of course when kids avoid taking responsibility for their actions, they hope to avoid the consequences. Eventually, mature children learn that taking responsibility may actually minimize the consequences they face. They admit hitting the garage door with the car, knowing that this will be easier than trying to pretend that the accident didn't happen.

In order to avoid consequences, adults deny responsibility too. Sometimes they do this by blaming someone else. Sometimes, they do this by avoiding the issue. Wanting to be always right, our pride keeps us from admitting our wrongs.

As humans, we adults tend to judge ourselves by our intentions. When we are stopped for speeding, we think that an important *excuse* for speeding will override the fact that we were actually driving faster than the speed limit. An overweight person overlooks how much he really ate by thinking about how much he restrained himself from having seconds.

When I'm trying to exercise more, I give myself credit for wanting to exercise—even on the days I don't make it to the gym.

Our pride keeps us from being honest with ourselves and with others.

Denying responsibility is part of the dark side of human nature. But for veterans, early military life taught us the importance of learning to deny culpability. For a career soldier, admitting mistakes (or getting caught in them) might mean the end of his career. Instead of admitting to bad planning, or the wrongful loss of troops, or the inadvertent death of civilians, officers learn to blame others, dispense misinformation, or to cover up their errors entirely.

The My Lai massacre, which took place on the morning of March 16, 1968, was a watershed in the history of modern American combat and a turning point in the public perception of the Vietnam War.

In the course of three hours, U.S. troops killed more than five hundred Vietnamese civilians in cold blood. The soldiers had been on a search and destroy mission to root out communist soldiers in fertile Viet Cong territory. Yet there had been no firefight with the enemy—not a single shot was fired at the soldiers of Charlie Company, a unit of the American's 11th Infantry Brigade.

Charlie Company's captain, Ernest Medina, who was on the ground at My Lai, realized he could not let news of the massacre reach the public. Though he had seen more than one hundred bodies, when questioned by a superior close to the scene, Medina maintained that gunship and artillery fire had killed no more than twenty to twenty-eight civilians.

His false testimony became the essence of a report submitted one month later by the commander of the 11th Infantry Brigade, Colonel Oran K. Henderson, who claimed that only twenty civilians had been inadvertently killed.

But the rumor mill, which began turning within days of My Lai, portrayed a very different story. Eventually, through the rumors and the work of one conscientious GI, who harbored ambitions to become a journalist, the allegations reached Washington politicians.

One year later, in spite of intense efforts to cover up the atrocity, the shocking story of the My Lai Massacre reached the newsstands.

Denying the truth seemed right for those involved.

Unfortunately, hiding the truth of My Lai only intensified the fallout and escalated the damage incurred by the military and the men involved. The American public could not forgive My Lai. And they would never forget that they could not trust their military or the American government. This break in faith continues to this very day, nearly thirty-five years later.

Unlike the military, healthy relationships depend on personal honesty.

There is another reason that veterans struggle with personal responsibility. And this is the darker, more difficult area to deal with.

I believe that every combat veteran holds within his soul a well of guilt. Deep inside, he knows that he has participated in the darkest part of human activity. He has killed.

Though his military activity was deemed necessary and considered morally correct, he cannot get away from the evil that he saw and participated in. He remembers the rush of combat, his almost animal willingness to participate in events too horrible to describe. He cannot share these realizations even with those he loves most.

The veteran keeps this well of truth—this bubbling cauldron of horror about himself—deeply hidden, carefully capped. He hides it from other humans—covering it with coping mechanisms like work, productivity, or worse, withdrawal, alcohol, and drugs.

This truth—the evil that the soldier has seen inside himself—is emotionally connected by a fragile thread to his responsibility in human interaction. To admit mistakes with his intimate partner is to open the valve to the deeper well of evil inside himself.

How can the soldier risk opening the valve? What would happen if all the evil inside him were to be seen by someone he loves? Wouldn't he be rejected? Why should he let anyone know about what lies inside? Nothing can be done for it anyway.

Desperate to keep the well capped, some soldiers refuse to admit responsibility for anything. While this technique may keep the truth from getting out, eventually it will destroy his relationships with those he loves.

The people closest to him soon recognize that the relationship cannot grow. Unless the combat veteran chooses to acknowledge his mistakes and move on, there is no hope for improvement or change.

In the context of the burn wound, keeping these dark truths hidden deep inside only allows them to fester—until they too bubble and boil with disease. In the end, this kind of disease can cause the death of relationships.

There is a better way.

BUILDING BRIDGES

1. Do you have difficulty admitting your own mistakes?
2. Do you harbor some feelings of guilt left over from the war? What have you done with those feelings? Have you justified your actions? Have you blamed your superiors? Your culture? Your government?
3. Does passing the blame ease your feelings of guilt?
4. What action do you most hope that no one ever discovers about you? Why do you feel that way? When was the last time you thought about this secret?

CHAPTER TWELVE

The End of the Beginning
(God Is Not American)

The journey into unrelieved darkness of the soul begins at that moment a person first discovers who he really is. The veneer of civilized behavior, smug feelings of righteousness, the naïve belief that all's well with the world can dissolve in a single instant of mad violence…Monstrous evil is no longer something he can attribute only to others. It is intrinsic to himself.

William P. Mahedy, *Out of the Night:*
The Spiritual Journey of Vietnam Vets

Have you ever known someone who is never wrong?

I once overheard a casual conversation where someone like that got caught with his facts out of line. Rather than admit his mistake, he went to elaborate—even laughable—lengths to get around his own error. I felt a little embarrassed for the guy. Having a relationship with him wouldn't be easy.

Only emotionally mature adults take personal responsibility for their own behavior. Sometimes, the course of our lives keeps us from growing up. Outside events combine to thwart our growth, keeping ordinary children from maturing into adults.

Some may have lived with an abusive parent. Each infraction brought inordinate, even dangerous consequences. For them, denying responsibility became a way of keeping punishment at bay. As a means of survival, these children learned to deflect their parent's attention by making certain someone else is found guilty. In doing so, they lived through another day.

Other children grew up in the overwhelming freedom of an overly-permissive parent. During their childhood, parents intervened for their every mistake. While trooping off to visit the school principal or the local police, these parents spewed complaints about the inadequacy of the world around them. By diverting responsibility, these parents kept their children out of every difficulty. These children learned to believe that the rest of the world *was* always at fault. Having never experienced the consequences of their own actions, blame and excuse-making became a habitual way of life.

These adults continue to believe that every negative consequence they experience is someone else's fault. They judge themselves by their own good intentions, using excuses like these: I didn't mean to be late. I didn't mean to yell.

Because they "didn't mean to" hurt us, they believe they have not.

While many learn to avoid responsibility as children, others develop a problem later in life. This is especially true for those who have experienced the profoundly abnormal world of war, or for those who have survived the life-threatening assault of another human. For these people, that one unaltered glimpse into the human soul—leaves their image of self and of their world permanently shattered.

Those of us who have survived know the truth.

We know what horrible evils humans are capable of. We know rage—an inner anger so deep that it rushes like a river through our soul, shearing away the banks of our humanity. We understand the burning desire for revenge. We know blood lust. We have seen, perhaps even in ourselves, a hatred so intense, so full of evil, that no justification for it can stand.

Having lived through the intense evils of war, we have experienced the truth—a truth about humanity that others may only suspect.

And we are left with a sort of aching sickness lying deep within us. Not knowing what it is, or what to do with it, we try to ignore it. We may try to drink it away, or work it away, or laugh it away. But it comes back—again and again—demanding our attention, sucking away our energy in a vague attempt to keep it covered up, beaten down, and shoved under.

The sensation gnaws at us. Sometimes, it feels like guilt—like getting caught with our hand in the cookie jar. Sometimes, it feels more vague. Sometimes, it feels so complex that we cannot define any part of it. As we give up and push the feeling away, we long instead for the simple misdemeanors of childhood.

This knowledge—this truth about human evil—lies tied up in our memories of the trauma we've experienced. Like asphalt, the individual ingredients are so melded together that they are no longer visible. Things we did. Things we saw. Things we didn't do. Things we wanted to do but couldn't. People we couldn't save.

People we might have saved, if only we'd known. People we might have saved if we hadn't been so afraid. Things we wanted to do, but fear held us back.

And with all this truth, the guilt settles into our souls like an occupying army. It begins to evolve into a living organism, a complex, many-sided thing. Like an octopus, it holds us firmly gripped. Though we long to escape, we cannot.

The truth that our trauma has taught us, about the unavoidable evil of man, lies in the middle of our gnawing guilt, flavoring the mixture with the taste of utter hopelessness. We are left with an unspeakable conclusion.

If man is evil, and I am man, then I too am guilty.

In the end we realize that evil isn't out there. It's in here—inside my own soul. No one can change that truth.

Even the less spiritual among us find the responsibility of that one statement overwhelming. This truth may be more than most of us are willing to face.

We know by experience that ignoring the truth will not make it go away. Patriotism—no matter how fervent—offers no solution. We find no relief in substance abuse, or prosperity, or success, or even in family.

We know instinctively that ordinary religion cannot relieve the intense pain of the truth. Pat answers and oversimplified explanations don't begin to confront the events we have survived, or the loss we have experienced.

God isn't an American. He didn't protect the good guys. Religious men experienced the same savage ferocity that all soldiers faced in Southeast Asia. He didn't protect all the Christian firemen who responded to the terrorist disaster in New York City. Good men died as the towers collapsed.

In ordinary religion, evil lies somewhere out there. Soldiers and survivors know better.

It does not help when well-meaning friends tell us, "You did what you had to." Or, "It was war. It doesn't count." Or, "You were afraid. Cut yourself some slack." In the deepest parts of our beings, we know better.

But what hope do we have for what we know?

You are not the first to discover the truth about humankind. Neither are you the only human to face this horrible truth about yourself. It appears as a dark cave, this journey into the truth of the soul. Appearances are deceiving. It is not a cave, but a tunnel, and as the old saying goes, there is light at the end of the tunnel.

You can be set free from the tentacles of guilt that drag you down.

The only way out of this tunnel is through it. Many veterans are still angry with God for their experiences in Vietnam. They believe that he abandoned them there. They resent his absence, his failure to protect them and their fellow soldiers. They resent the injustice of the war, the futility of the cause, the failure of the government to make good on its promises to our soldiers during and after the war. Deep anger over these issues still boils in the hearts of many veterans.

The same is true of men who survived the terrorist attacks in New York. In the CBS documentary filmed during the Trade Center disaster, Battalion Chief Joseph Pfeifer of the Number 7 Engine Company lost his brother in the collapse of tower number one. At the end of the film, he says this, "We used to love doing this job. We loved being downtown. We loved being firefighters. And now I don't love it anymore."

In the terrorist attacks on the NYC Trade Towers, Chief Pfeifer lost more than his brother, he lost the joy he once felt every day—the joy of a job he loved, the joy of the city he served. An innocent man lost a huge part of his life because of a brutal attack committed by strangers.

He has a right to be angry about losing his brother.

For most of us who survive trauma, our anger becomes misdirected. We are angry that God is not who we believed him to be—that he did not operate on our agenda. That he is not an American God. That he did not side with our soldiers, with the good guys, with our friends. That he did not somehow prevent the terrible and undeserved attacks of September 11. That he did not stop the drunk who drove head-on into our daughter's car.

And in our anger, we fail to see that we have formed a God of our own making. He should act like this, we think. He should feel like this, we believe. And rather than facing the reality of the living God, we face the intense disappointment of our own idol—a God we have fashioned in our own image—who will not deliver the solutions we expect.

To get through this dilemma, we must start over. We must throw out the image of God that we have carefully crafted from our wishful imagination. No matter where we grew up, or what congregation we were part of, we must face the reality of a God who is not content to live in the tiny box we make for him.

He insists on being God.

God is not American. He does not control men. He does not stop us from making our own bullets and then standing others in front of them. He is God.

And that is enough.

In fact, this discovery—that man is capable of unspeakable evil (in fact that I *myself* am capable of such evil) is not new to God. He is not surprised by it. The truth does not inhibit his ability to be God. In fact, he said it long before we first had the thought.

> All have turned away. Together everyone has become useless. There is no one who does anything good; there is not even one. Their throats are like open graves; they use their tongues for telling lies. Their words are like snake poison. Their mouths are full of cursing and hate. They are always ready to kill people…They have no fear of God. (Romans 3:12-18 NCV)

You can console yourself knowing that God completely agrees with what you have discovered about yourself, about your country, about your superiors and others in Vietnam. He agrees with your assessment of terrorists, of criminals and of sexual predators. There is a problem and *we are the problem*—not God.

The desolation, guilt, and loneliness you feel down in the pit of your soul are only the results of the problem—symptoms if you will. They are not the problem itself.

This inside evil wants to keep us from the only thing that can help us.

I like this passage from a very old part of the Bible:

> Surely the Lord's power is enough to save you. He can
> hear you when you ask him for help. It is your evil that has
> separated you from God. Your sins cause him to turn away
> from you so he does not hear you. (Isaiah 59:1-2 NCV)

What hope do we have if God himself no longer will listen to us? If our evil nature serves to separate us from him, what can we do? Where can we turn? How can we get God to listen and respond to us?

He has made a way.

In fact, his way is to go through the same dark tunnel himself and to serve the sentence for our evil.

Be careful. This is not religion. It is not denominational. This solution does not depend on your understanding. Jesus—himself God—took the form of a man and came into our world. He experienced for himself the hatred and jealously and evil of men. Though he was innocent, he was murdered. Though he'd done nothing worthy of death, he was nailed to a cross. And in so doing, an innocent man took the full penalty for our sins—all our sins.

Even your sins. Even the ones you have yet to commit.

We do not need to sort them, or to categorize them. We don't need to know which ones we might have avoided, or which we committed because we were under orders. We don't need to quantify how much of what we did was due to fear or incompetence or selfishness. He paid the penalty for every evil thing we ever did—whether we knew it was evil or not; whether we were under orders or not; whether we were frightened out of our wits or not.

He took them all. He paid the full penalty for every one of our mistakes. By his death, we obtain a full pardon from God. Forgiveness is a free gift from God.

In his death, he made the way for us to be free of the weight of guilt. But more than that, his death and resurrection frees us from the very evil which is our nature.

Because of his resurrection, we have the opportunity to turn things around. Though we know evil lives inside us, it need not control us. We can tap into a new power, a power outside of ourselves.

God offers to live inside us—a kind of "alternative fuel source," giving us whatever we need to live a new life, a life of love and gentleness and peace. This peace, which comes from God, is not the peace of men or of governments but a peace within our souls. It can never be taken from us.

In Vietnam, we sought to *defeat* the enemy.

But in the war of the soul, *we must surrender.*

In a book about relationships, what relationship is more important that your relation with your creator? God wants to know and love and care for you.

Think about it. You can surrender to the maker of your soul. You can have the gift of peace—a kind of peace that can never be taken from you. You can have the power to make new choices. You can begin to build new relational bridges with the people around you.

By taking this step, you can finally accept responsibility for the small things in your relationships, knowing that the really big things—the things you've been hiding in your soul for years—have already been taken care of. His sacrifice—Jesus' death on your behalf—gives you the ability to admit your mistakes.

You can be wrong, because there is forgiveness for every wrong. You can admit mistakes, because you have a new source of power to turn away from your mistakes.

He paid the price for you to be free. No one can make the choice for you.

I made the choice after coming home in 1986.

I was at a point in my life that the stress, insomnia, and depression got the best of me. I broke down and called a friend who had been a paratrooper in the Korean War. When he answered his phone I simply said, "Bill, I need a friend right now."

He was quiet for a moment and then replied, "Chuck, you need the Lord."

His response surprised me. A week earlier I might have laughed at his comment, but at this particular moment, my life was in shambles. God waited a long time for me to get to this needy, desperate point. Like a lifeguard waits until a drowning man stops flailing so he can save him, Jesus stood by and waited for me to stop trying to survive by my own means. He waited until I gave up. Only then could I rely solely on him. It was time for this soldier to surrender—a practice foreign to those who serve in the world's army.

I straightened up in my chair, brushed away tears I had not shed in almost twenty years, and heard myself say, "Yeah, yeah, that's one thing I haven't tried…maybe that's what I need to do."

Then my friend said something else. He asked me if I was willing to pray with him about it. I agreed because I knew my life needed an overhaul. I'd run out of answers. I also knew that my own plans had only brought disaster and more grief for everyone.

That afternoon, I prayed with Bill and gave my heart, soul, and life to the Lord Jesus Christ.

When I got off the phone, I didn't hear angels singing or rockets going off, but I felt different. I didn't have a glitzy religious experience, but I sensed a kind of peace that I hadn't ever felt, a sense of release far beyond any drug or "method" I'd tried before.

As time went on, the heavy symptoms of PTSD began to fall away. The memories felt like another part of a life that I had once lived. Day by day the nightmares and horrible mental images that had hounded me all those years diminished. It was as if Jesus was taking all of these troubled mental pictures from my subconscious mind and mounting them in a photo album. I could still see them from time to time, but they no longer held the same power over me they once had.

I would never go back. Maybe you shouldn't either.

You could make the same decision I did. You could do it today.

Building Bridges

1. Are you haunted by the horrible evil you experienced?
2. Are you aware of a kind of evil in yourself? Can you identify some of the behaviors this evil encourages in you?
3. Do you want to be free of the pull of evil in your soul?
4. Would you consider letting God take care of the evil you cannot control? Why not?
5. Do you know a Christian who would talk about this issue with you?
6. If you are ready try this prayer:

God, I surrender. I agree with your assessment. I have done things my own way. I have left you out of my life. I've made my own decisions and tried to solve my own problems. But God, I'm the problem. I need your help. I believe that you sent your Son, Jesus to take the penalty for my stubborn selfishness. I believe you can set me free from the power of evil inside me. I accept that freedom, Lord. And I accept the gift of eternal life that comes with faith in Jesus. I give you my whole life, God, not just the good parts. I give you the whole thing. Take me, Lord, and change me into the man you want me to be. I surrender to you. Amen.

CHAPTER THIRTEEN

Marriage—
an Endurance Race

The terrorists who acted on September 11 were betting that our American society is brittle. They hoped such a calamity would not only topple buildings and kill thousands but that their efforts would upend the entire nation. To preserve the stability of families in the face of that kind of stress will require spouses to find an inner reserve of strength that will allow them to ride out this national tragedy.

Michael Angelo, *Business News*, October 2001

S tatistically, many survivors of trauma experience broken marriages. Having survived an assault of the soul, (whether by natural disaster, auto accident, criminal acts, or the trauma of war) survivors find themselves exhausted, distracted, and struggling to return to normal life.

Angelo (quoted above) rightly sensed the effect of tragedy on marriages. Through no fault of their own, both partners find that their relationship has unalterably changed. They wonder if things can ever be the same again.

The healthy partner wonders, *Will my partner survive this trauma? Will I ever again enjoy the person I married?* The survivor wonders, *Will this injury cripple me forever?* Both may wonder if genuine love will return to the relationship.

Unfortunately, many marriages don't survive. Some victims find themselves single again at a time when they most need the unconditional love of another human.

What can people do when faced with this kind of trauma? What can we expect from the institution of marriage? How can we insure that our marriage will survive the assaults of the past and the traumas we have yet to experience?

ENDURANCE

I ride a bike. Not just to the store to pick up a few things…I ride a lot. In fact, not long ago, I rode the two hundred miles between Seattle, Washington and Portland, Oregon in just two days.

Two hundred miles in two days.

As I trained for the trip, I read a few bicycling books. I learned about the importance of nutrition, the need for gradually increasing distance on my training rides, and for adequate rest between rides. The human body, as it turns out, is a complex entity. Expecting the body to endure such abuse without excellent care guarantees failure.

Most experts agree that building muscle strength begins by breaking down muscle tissue. We do that by exercising just slightly beyond our level of comfort. The added stress makes micro-tears in the muscle tissue—actual areas of measurable damage. Sounds destructive doesn't it? Who'd expect strength to come from demolition?

As it turns out, the body responds to these micro tears by building tissue more impervious to abuse. As the body works to increase its resistance to the stress of exercise, the muscle becomes stronger. The strength remains as long as the muscle continues to be stressed by exercise. As exercise intensity is increased, the cycle begins again.

Stress. Rest. Recovery. Strength. This is the documented pattern of strength building in muscles.

Enduring marriages follow a similar pattern. Even as relationships progress through predictable phases of development, they also cycle through a series of assaults. Some of these—like buying a house—can be fairly pleasant. Others—like the sudden death of a child—can be overwhelming. But some traumas, especially those experienced by only one of the partners (like rape, car accidents, assault) can shake the very foundation of the relationship.

While some couples spend their lives avoiding assaults, others face them with confidence. These couples know that trouble, like exercise, makes a marriage stronger. A strong marriage doesn't simply materialize the moment you say the vows, place the ring on the finger, and kiss one another in front of friends and families—no more than strong legs appear on the day you buy your first road bike.

On the wedding day, most couples have nothing more than a promise and a hope.

Most newlyweds haven't experienced any real stress. Two people in a new relationship, based largely on physical attraction and the euphoria of head-over-heels infatuation know very little about one another. When we date, we smell good, comb our hair, wear our best clothes, and use our best "company manners."

When couples finally agree to marry, reality hits home.

He has mood swings. She likes to wear sweat pants and wool socks to bed. He never records his checks in the check register. She hates having company. Reality begins with irritations.

Unless both partners are willing to work through the irritations, the relationship can begin to flounder.

At this point, many observers begin to use the "C" word. Commitment, they say, is the glue that holds marriages together.

And while commitment will hold a marriage together, it doesn't guarantee that the relationship will reach its full potential. If commitment is the only glue involved, neither partner will ever discover the best in themselves or their partner.

A marriage held together by grit alone is as vulnerable as a rock wall. It will stand—but not with the strength of a well-engineered concrete wall with a strong foundation, lots of rebar and well-planned deadheads.

Before a connection between a man and woman can develop into a strong life partnership, some pretty heavy emotional terrain must be navigated. If you aren't ready for the unavoidable bumps along the way, your relationship may suffer.

It all comes down to being prepared.

So how do we look ahead and see what we will encounter along the way? Well, surprisingly enough, the patterns of marriage are pretty predictable. In general terms, we can give you some idea of the different stages that your marriage will go through (or has gone through already). Anticipating the route will make it easier to handle the dips and curves along the path.

Remember: dips and curves are unavoidable. How you handle them is up to you. Here's one way to chart your way through your marriage relationship:

PHASE ONE: FEELINGS

Every relationship begins with an emphasis on one another's physical presence—the electricity and excitement men and women get from being with and physically touching each other. At this stage two people overlook one another's faults, shortcomings, or differences. Their decisions are mostly based on sizzle and feelings. At this point, emotions often sweep two people into marriage.

A connection tip: The magic of the new husband-wife relationship can wear off in as little as ninety days. Sometimes the thrill lasts longer. But whenever Phase One starts to fade, remember the marriage is not failing—the time has come to change and adjust. You only need to recognize that you are about to move into Phase Two.

PHASE TWO: SECOND THOUGHTS

Suddenly, that sock left hanging on the lamp in the bedroom is no longer a euphoric reminder of last night's warm touch. In the cold light of day, those socks prove what you've come to believe—you married a slob! At this point your sexual attraction seems to sputter, making matters even worse.

As reality sets in, the differences, faults, shortcomings, and disagreements seem to surface all at once. Suddenly, that cute little grin your mate had in Phase One has become a crooked mouth, and you wonder if you've married a mutant.

This phase can be complicated by the need to make life-changing decisions: Should we have kids? Should we buy a home? What does the financial future like? These decisions and the answers the couple pursues can bring additional stress and change to the relationship.

Here you may say to yourself: *What was I thinking? Why did I marry this person?*

Don't let your doubts overcome your courage! Facing these irritations and disappointments will strengthen your marriage muscle. As you navigate these decisions and find middle ground, your ability to connect and to meet one another's real needs deepens.

A connection tip: Accept the fact that disagreements are inevitable (and normal). Ruth Bell Graham, wife of evangelist Billy Graham, says it like this, "If both of us agree on everything, one of us is no longer necessary."

This might be a time to consider taking a class on conflict resolution—with both parties attending. Don't let your differences lead you to isolation. Pursue common activities and interests.

Make time to play together. Laugh frequently. Close communication is imperative at this point. Spend time together.

Think of your relationship like a savings account. If disagreements are like withdrawals, then time together is like a deposit. You have to have money in the account to cover the withdrawals. Otherwise, you'll get an overdraft notice in the form of divorce papers. In spite of the pressure to establish your career, or start a family, make your marriage your first priority. Investments in your relationship at this stage will inoculate your relationship from the damage inflicted by the stages and conflicts that are yet to be overcome.

Phase Three: *Who Changes?*

I don't know how many times I have wanted my spouse to change to fit my scheme of things. In fact, I used to pray for God to make her change according to my expectations. But this phase is not about changing my partner as much as it is about changing me.

At this phase the stress generated by disagreement has the potential to drive two people apart. The same stress can also drive both persons toward growth. Only you can make this very personal decision for yourself.

Ask yourself what you can do to grow in this phase. How can you be a better partner? How can you be a more caring person? How can you become a more mature individual? How can you face and overcome your own imperfections?

In this phase, you can learn to accept your partner exactly as they are. This will be easier if you spend time every day looking for and acknowledging your partner's good points. Keep your partner's strengths in mind as you deal with the weaknesses in your relationship.

A connection tip: Communication in Phase Three must be completely honest while at the same time kind and considerate. Both partners must deal with feelings, opinions, and facts. Working to solve problems must be done together. If you want to solve problems on your own, you may soon be living that way—alone. Consider the problem, not your partner, as your *mutual* enemy. For your relationship to win, you must fight on the same team against an outside threat.

Phase Four: Settle In

In this stage couples that have weathered the rocky parts of the relationship settle-in. They believe that they will be able to work out their future together. They have made the Phase Three changes in themselves, and each partner recognizes (and even finds humor) in their differences and disagreements.

Couples who have settled in finally understand and have learned to accept the good with the bad. They appreciate one another's idiosyncrasies. Their relationship has years of shared history, and they have become the epitome of "family."

A connection tip: Don't let acceptance become a cover for complacency. When problems arise, continue to work together to solve them. Always communicate your affirmation that you will be there for your partner no matter what. Continue to encourage and appreciate your partner. Invest in your relationship with the same determination that you invest in your retirement. Stay healthy to enjoy the fruit of your labor.

Remember the muscles:

As you work your way through these phases, you will find yourselves facing the same kinds of challenges that muscles face. There will be periods of stress (the death of a parent, the loss of a job, an unexpected illness) that demand changes in the relationship. This demand for change has the potential to damage the relationship. Conversely, like exercise strengthens a well-trained muscle, stress has potential to strengthen the relationship.

You and your partner have the ability to choose. Which will it be? Damage or strength?

Don't forget to enjoy one another and let your relationship flourish in the periods of rest and recovery. Some couples get so busy accumulating or accomplishing, that they let the relatively quiet periods go by without reconnecting with their partner. When the next stressful event occurs, they have no strength to withstand the assault.

During times of stress, draw together. Battle the enemy together. Determine to let the battle itself make your relationship stronger.

During times of rest, enjoy one another. Deepen your ties. Relax in your love for one another. You will be rested, stronger, and ready for the next battle.

Use your commitment toward your partner to triumph over the adversity you face together. Know that your relationship will have periods of stress and trouble. Every relationship does.

But if you can work *together* to solve the problems, your relationship will grow. There is nothing more satisfying than the fruit of a lifelong partnership with another human who knows everything there is to know about you, and loves you anyway.

BUILDING BRIDGES

1. If you are married, in what phase of marriage do you currently find yourself?
2. How have you responded to stress in the past? Has it made you stronger? How?
3. Can you think of a time when stress brought you closer to your partner? Could you talk about it together? What made that stress different than other, more destructive stresses?
4. If you've had a prior marriage, can you name the stress that finally overcame the strength of your marriage?

Knowing that marriages have tidal actions, ups and downs, what might you have done differently during that last period of stress? How might you have faced the stress while strengthening the relationship?

5. What strengths did you take away from that previous marriage? Did that final blow leave you with new weaknesses or handicaps? What are they? Do you have the courage to ask your friends how they might answer the same question?

6. What skill would you like to develop to help your marriage grow stronger right now?

7. How could you begin to work on that skill?

CHAPTER FOURTEEN

Victory Is Possible

*Our brothers won the victory over him by the blood of the
Lamb and by the truth which they proclaimed; and they
were willing to give up their lives and die.*

Revelation 12:11

S o far, we've discussed the importance of staying connected
with other humans. We've looked at the ways trauma sepa-
rates us from those we love. We've talked about ways to work
through conflict and build intimacy. We've talked about the importance of taking control of our self-talk. But even with so many
tools in your relational toolbox, you still face the most important
choice of your life. What will you do about your relationships?

This is a choice that only you can make.

Connections never flourish by accident.

When I wrote *Nam Vet, Making Peace with Your Past* (first
published in 1987), I wrote mostly from my own experience.
Though I sensed that others had suffered in the same way that I

had, I didn't really know the extent of damage done to other Vietnam vets by their experiences in Southeast Asia. In the nearly twenty years since I wrote that first book, I have accumulated hundreds of accounts of men and women haunted by their war-time experiences.

The extent of the damage is as individual as the men and women who survived the war. Yet in many ways the nature of the damage is the same.

Even today, I am astounded by the similarity of struggles experienced by those who survive trauma. Whether by nature, by war, or by the evil acts of men, trauma leaves its mark on the human soul. And though the traumatic event may end, our suffering doesn't go away when the wind stops blowing or the police sirens fade or when we find ourselves back home in our American living room.

I'm only beginning to accept the fact that the war will always be with me. After so many years of trying to forget, followed by years of working to "get over it," I know that Vietnam has become a part of the fabric of my life. It has been a hard part, yes, but an integral part.

Some veterans say that Vietnam has made them who they are.

I would put it this way: My Vietnam experience has forced me to make choices. Because of Vietnam, I chose Jesus. That choice and many others have helped me to grow a kind of strength, character, and perseverance I would never have any other way.

Would I volunteer to do it again? No. I would not volunteer for a combative role again. But I would certainly honor my duty to country in a care-giving capacity. At the same time, I refuse to throw away the very gifts that this suffering has brought to my life. If God directs me to help give life or save lives, I am willing to use these gifts as he directs.

I can keep the things I have learned to myself, or I can choose to share them with others through relationships. In fact, more than anything, I want to share what I have discovered. One of the ways I do that has been through my relationships with other veterans through Point Man International.

Through Point Man, I've attended weekly meetings where I've learned to trust other men again. I've been able to go through my "stuff" at my own pace, knowing that I won't be criticized or judged. Some weeks, I just listen. At other times, I'll try to verbalize some of the stuff I've struggled with all of these long years. Those guys will listen to me, no matter what I have to say. They've never given up on me—no matter how crazy I may sound.

While Point Man is a Christian ministry, no one hits anyone over the head with the Bible. They don't try to shame guys into agreeing with their philosophy. Instead they've offered me respect and friendship and genuine love. In the hothouse of love, healing has no choice but to grow and blossom.

What I'm trying to say is that the ability to have and maintain healthy relationships depends on our willingness to go through our own rucksack of trauma. We do that in healthy relationships like the vet group or in other groups—like Adult Children of Alcoholics, or a Twelve Steps group. Some of us have to do it in the safety of a professional counselor's office. Ironically, as we work with others—be it one other person or twelve—in the group setting, our other safe and healthy relationships will begin to thrive.

I'd like to share some of the letters I've gotten from other veterans who have worked through these issues.

Richard wrote this:

> When I returned home from Vietnam, I put everything behind me...I was home, and I was going to take a long R&R. I also wanted to have some fun...Eventually, I was partied-out, and reality hit me smack in the face. I was absolutely miserable! I was lonely; I had nobody to love and nobody who would love me in return. What good was surviving Vietnam if a life of loneliness was all I had to look forward to?

...The years turned into meaninglessness as I fulfilled the typical role of husband and father with less and less dedication or affection. My temper was getting worse; my anger was always violent. I began to drink more beer, smoke more pot, and look at more young single girls. I felt like I was under the influence of some negative force that was intent on destroying my marriage. The last thing I wanted was to be a failure at the very thing I wanted most out of life; a family of my own. I found myself unable to do those things which I knew I should, or avoid doing the things that I knew I shouldn't be doing. Once again I was a miserable man.

Richard made a decision, not unlike the one I made years after I came home from Vietnam. He recognized the evil forces taking over his life. He put it this way:

> Something evil was at work. It was clearly more than mental illness, or the desperation of a religious fanatic. This something evil was definitely the enemy of God, out to destroy his creation and slander his good name.

Though he had survived Vietnam, Richard had entered a far more deadly war. This invisible enemy wanted to defeat him and to destroy his life. Instead, he surrendered to Jesus Christ. The change in his life was not instantaneous; but it was miraculous.

> The years have turned to joy. My marriage has been restored, my daughters are now beautiful teens, and God has blessed me with the last thing I could have asked him for, a son.

Dave, who served in Vietnam as a medic speaks of his isolation this way:

As my life went on, and Vietnam was over, it still lived inside of me, strong as ever. The nightmares kept coming back and haunting me, and the pain was always there. I couldn't find the peace that I kept looking for, so the drugs were the only way for relief. When I was high there was no pain, but I was still filled with anger and rage with no end in sight. I couldn't get close to anyone. Nor did I let anyone get close to me. I wouldn't let them, I was alone, but Vietnam still lived in me. Even though it hurt, I liked it. I went through life unloving, caring about no one.

Eventually, Dave came to the end of his resources. Arriving at a city bus stop, he called the only man who had ever cared for him. This veteran took him to a Point Man meeting where Dave finally experienced the safety of other men who'd been through the same agony. Those men convinced Dave to give God a chance. Now, having surrendered his life to Jesus, he has a new sense of peace and happiness he'd never before thought possible. The drugs and alcohol are gone, and Dave moved on to attend seminary. Now in place of isolation, Dave is helping people—all kinds of people—find new life in Jesus Christ.

Perhaps the best story of reconciliation comes from one of my close friends, Bob Silveria, a Vietnam vet, active in Point Man Ministries. Bob came home from the Nam hooked on adrenaline. After marrying, having a daughter, and being asked to resign after a stint in law enforcement, Bob became a trip wire vet, living alone in the Canadian Rocky Mountains. Eventually, he returned to civilization, though his addictions to cocaine and alcohol kept him from living a normal life.

Bob was miserable. He considered taking his own life, going so far as to put a gun to his head. But at that crucial moment, Bob found he had no courage to pull the trigger.

When a favorite uncle died suddenly, Bob decided to attend the funeral services in California. His ex-wife picked him up at the airport, and on a whim, Bob decided to attend church with her. There, he had a most remarkable experience.

During the course of the service, by a powerful moving of the Holy Spirit, Bob saw what a mess he'd made of his life. He saw his own inability to change the direction he'd chosen, and recognized his need for divine forgiveness. The force of the Holy Spirit was so strong that Bob surrendered his life to God and accepted forgiveness in Jesus Christ.

Bob started a new life.

In his own words, Bob describes that day, "I can't explain it—but that morning, I was completely delivered from the drug and alcohol addictions. It was gone. I had no desire at all to return to the life I'd lived."

But the miracle didn't end there. After years of struggling with deep loneliness and recurrent isolation, Bob's life began another change. He began reaching out to other veterans. At the same time, he began reshaping his relationship with his wife. Six months after that church service, Bob and Barb Silveria were remarried. He began to build a relationship with his daughter, which until then had hardly existed. Today, Bob and Barb work actively helping other veterans.

I could fill these pages with dozens of examples of Vietnam veterans who have overcome the isolation of trauma and regained their connections with others in the human race. But what about survivors of other traumatic events?

Consider the story of Jerry Schemmel, survivor of an airplane crash into an Iowa cornfield. When Jerry stepped onto Flight 232 in Denver, Colorado headed for Chicago, he had all the confident trappings of a successful professional life. One hour after take off, an explosion destroyed one of the aircraft engines and rendered the entire hydraulics system useless. For the next fifty-four minutes, the passengers of Flight 232 faced certain death.

During the moments between the explosion of the rear engine and the beginning of the fiery slide down the Sioux City runway, Jerry went through monumental fear and deep introspection. He penned a note about his insurance coverage and put it into his briefcase. He considered his love for his wife and the grief she would undoubtedly endure. Moments later, in the confusion and darkness of a twisted, smoking cabin, a single shaft of sunlight provided Jerry's only guide to safety. Somehow, in the confusion, he managed to escape carrying a small infant with him.

Miraculously, Jerry survived the crash that killed nearly half of the plane's passengers. But his closest friend did not.

Though Jerry's body survived, his psyche seemed severely, irreparably damaged. His slide from shock to depression and from depression to self-pity nearly ended his marriage with his wife, Diane. He puts his torment this way, "Not one day passes that I don't consider the experience, if only for a moment in the morning while looking into the bathroom mirror, and feel its reverberations."

But Jerry didn't give up. He didn't let the isolation take his life—the life which had been so miraculously spared. Jerry, like Bob Silveria and myself, came to a place where he surrendered his past to God. Then, with care and time, he rebuilt the life he shared with Diane.

Now, Jerry is the play-by-play announcer for the NBA Denver Nuggets. He is a favorite motivational speaker, and you can read the whole story in his book *Chosen to Live*.

These stories all convey a central point—one I want you to consider before you close the cover of this book. You too are a survivor. You were chosen to survive the trauma that you experienced.

I can't explain why God chooses some to survive and others to die. Though I understand that we must all die at some point in time, I don't know how God determines how many days each of us will enjoy upon the earth.

But I do know this: *you are alive today*. And it is up to you to choose how you will live the rest of your days. You can choose to remain one of the living dead—empty, purposeless, alone. Or you can choose to live—to really live.

No one can force you to choose life.

But I can offer this one observation. You've made it this far. You want something more. Go for it. Don't let anything—not guilt, depression, isolation, loneliness, substance abuse, alcohol, fear, or anger—ANYTHING keep you from living the rest of your life connected to others.

Your closest connections give you courage. They can help you when you are weak. They can love you when you are unlovable. They can help you find direction and strength. They can support you as you face trials. God often uses people to express his deep and unfailing love for us. Why choose to live a solitary and empty life, when so much wealth lies at your fingertips?

You went through trauma. You survived. Now, get connected.

Choose to *really* live.

ENDNOTES

CHAPTER TWO

1. Diane Guernsey, "Healthily Ever After," *Town and Country*, August 1999, V153, Page 112

2. Diane Guernsey, "Healthily Ever After," *Town and Country* August 1999, V153, Page 112

3. Barbara Foley Wilson and Charlotte Schoenborn, "A Healthy Marriage," *American Demographics*, November 1989, V11, i11, Page 40

4. Cheryl Wetzstein, "For Better or Best," *Insight on the News*, November 27, 2000, V16, i44, Page 26

5. Diane Gurensey, "Healthily Ever After," *Town and Country*, August 1999, Page 112

6. Bruce Bower, "Social Life Nothing to Sneeze At," *Science News*, July 1997, V152, i1, Page 11

7. Oystrein Kravdal, "Impact of Marital Status on Cancer Survival," *Journal of Social Science and Medicine*, Feb 2001, V53, i3, Page 357

8. Paula England, "The Case for Marriage: Why Married People Are Happier Healthier and Better off Financially," *Contemporary Sociology*, Volume 30, Page 564

9. Ted Olsen, "For Better or Worse," *Christianity Today*, April 1, 2002, V46, i14, Page 22

CHAPTER THREE

1. Dr. John Gottman, "What Makes Marriage Work?" *Psychology Today*, V27, i2, Page 38

2. Riggs, Byrne, Weathers, and Litz, "The Quality of Intimate Relationships of Male Vietnam Veterans: Problems Associated with Post-Traumatic Stress Disorder," *Journal of Post Traumatic Stress*, Jan 1998, V11, i1, Page 87-101

3. Tiffany Danitz, "Drowning the Demons of War," *Insight on the News*, March 3 1997, V13, i8, Page 14

CHAPTER FIVE

1. Bill Hewitt, William Calley, (My Lai Massacre Convict), *People Weekly*, November 20, 1989, V32, i21, Page 152

For further information on support and
assistance for veterans and their loved
ones contact us: www.namvetbook.com

Or call Point Man International
Ministries hotline at 1-800-877-VETS

When the War Is Over...A New One Begins
Order Form

Please send *When the War Is Over...A New One Begins* **to:**

Name: _____

Address: _____

City: _____ State: _____

Zip: _____

Telephone: (_____) _____

Book Price: $11.99

Shipping: $3.00 for the first book and $1.00 for each additional book to cover shipping and handling within US, Canada, and Mexico. International orders add $6.00 for the first book and $2.00 for each additional book.

Order from:
Pine Hill Graphics
85334 Lorane Hwy
Eugene, OR 97405

1-866-301-READ

Or contact your local bookstore